Moon City Review 2012

Special Volume in Contemporary Children's Literature

T0308879

Муха ЦК

Муха, Муха ЦК Туха-
чевский командарм
Съездил мухе по мордам,
А Луначарский наркомпрос
Вызвал муху на допрос.

Moon City Review 2012

Special Volume in Contemporary Children's Literature

Editors Joel D. Chaston and Linda Trinh Moser

Missouri State University

moon city press
springfield missouri
2012

www.mooncitypress.com

An earlier version of "Counsel for 'Babees': Fathers, Mothers, and Early Advice Books for Children" appeared in *The Lion and the Unicorn* 29.1 (2004): 52-61. We thank the journal editors for permission to reuse materials.

"My Joke About a Worm," a song from the young adult novel, *The Hoarders* (Springville, UT: Cedar Fort, 2010), and "All I Want," a song from the novel, *Balance* (Springville, UT: Cedar Fort, 2011), are reprinted from Jean Stringam's author website, jeanstringamauthor.wordpress.com. We thank her for permission to include these pieces.

Cover Design and Interior Layout: Eric Pervukhin
Copy Editing: Karen Craigo

ISBN 13: 978-0-913785-36-2

Moon City Review 2012:
Special Volume in Contemporary Children's Literature

II. Beasts and Fabulous Creatures

Joel D. Chaston

Introduction

As I am writing the introduction to this special volume of *Moon City Review,* several recent articles in national newspapers have commented on a so-called revitalization of the publishing industry sparked by the popularity of best-selling children's and young adult series, such as J.K. Rowling's *Harry Potter* books (1997-2007) and Suzanne Collins's *Hunger Games* trilogy (2008-2010), which, while originally targeted at young readers, have attracted a large adult audience. During the same time, Oscar-winning film director Danny Boyle gave equal time to Shakespeare and characters from British children's books (Peter Pan, Mary Poppins, Lord Voldemort) in the Opening Ceremonies he staged for the 2012 Summer Olympics in London. Boyle has explained that he believes British children's literature is one of his country's greatest national treasures.

The influence of children's and young adult literature on popular literature is immense, although many scholars disagree on its value and, more importantly, what we really mean by "children's literature." As Beverly Lyon Clark notes in *Kiddie Lit: The Cultural Construction of Children's Literature* (2003), the term "children's literature" is often confusing and problematic. Clark poses the question, "Where else could one find a body of literature in which virtually none of those who write it, none of those who edit or publish or market it, and very few of those who buy it, belong to its ostensible audience?" (14). Like many contemporary scholars of children's literature, Clark notes that status of children's literature as well as the "positioning of children and childhood in the American imagination has changed over the last two centuries," becoming more segregated "from adults and adulthood" due to a "split between high culture and low" (16).

In many ways, *Moon City Review 2012* responds to the question, "What is children's literature?" through fiction, poetry, drama, essays, and art

written for and/or about children and young adults. Many of the selections in this volume are targeted directly at young audiences, while others dialogue with earlier children's texts by revising or reimagining them for adult audiences. We have chosen to view the term "literature" broadly, including traditional literary forms—fiction, poetry, drama—along with songs, drawings, paintings, and photographs. Through the use of full-color illustrations and embellishments, we have tried to create a volume which, at times, captures the feel of an illustrated children's book.

In this volume, we have grouped the selections into five thematic sections, each of which includes a variety of subgenres of children's literature. The offerings in Section One, "Songs of Innocence," like William Blake's *Songs of Innocence* (1789), focus on the "innocence" of early childhood. "Sleep Anywhere," an image by Eleanor Leonne Bennett, a sixteen-year-old, award-winning photographer from the United Kingdom, sets the tone for this section with a child who might be playing hide-and-seek in a tree or bush. "David Chewed His Fingernails" and "That's When I Knew," the first of two groups of poems in this collection by David Harrison (author of seventy-seven books), humorously explore epiphanies in the lives of young children, as do Donna Barkman's "Elizabeth" and Mandi Reed's "The Great Button Chase," stories targeted at directly at younger readers. Judith Gero John's critical essay, "Counsel For 'Babees': Fathers, Mothers, and Early Advice Books For Children," explores adult attitudes towards childhood as expressed in early advice books produced for children moving into adulthood.

Section Two, "Beasts and Fabulous Creatures," explores topics that appear frequently in oral tales and fables and have inspired many contemporary children's stories and poems. In the tradition of allegorical animal fantasies, such as George Orwell's *Animal Farm* (1945) and Art Speiglman's *Maus: A Survivor's Tale* (1991), Eric Pervukhin's images of mice, along with Julie Platt's poems inspired by them, infuse beast fables and nursery rhymes with political and adult subtexts, simultaneously addressing adults and children. Chad Woody's "The Honest Trout" and

12

"The Robot Who Attended Mardi Gras" and Shelli McGrath's "An Unprecedented Surplus of Noselings" feature anthropomorphic animals and machines in humorous modern tall tales and fables.

We are grateful to the Missouri State University Library's Special Collections and Archives for access to Robert Wallace's unpublished manuscript *Full Alphabet* (1993), which includes a selection revised from his *Critters* (1978), a collection of poems about imaginary creatures. In his essay, "The Intersection of Fantasy and Social Commentary in Roald Dahl's *Fantastic Mr. Fox*," Mark I. West, author of *Roald Dahl* (Twayne, 1992), provides an insightful critical introduction to one of Dahl's animal fantasies. Finally, with the assistance of David O'Neill, great-nephew of Rose O'Neill and director of the Rose O'Neill Museum in Springfield, Missouri, we are privileged to reproduce artwork and verse by Rose O'Neill, featuring her fabulous creatures—the still-influential and popular Kewpies, which, like much Golden Age children's literature, are subversive in their elevation of children over adults.

Fantasy and adventure-romances inspired by traditional folktales, myths, and hero tales are among the most popular forms of children's literature. The stories and poems in Section Three, "Rewritings and Revisions," like much contemporary writing for the young, are intertextual—conversing with and, at times, revising earlier texts intended for readers of the authors' own day. Angelia Northrip-Rivera's essay on Lewis Carroll's *Alice's Adventures in Wonderland* (1865) and *Through the Looking-Glass and What Alice Found There* (1871) responds to Golden Age children's texts which, in turn, imitated and reimagined earlier books for the young. Young E. Allison's "Derelict" (1891) expands upon a song-snippet from Robert Louis Stevenson's *Treasure Island* (1883); itself a response to previous literature, Allison's sea shanty is revisited in turn by visual artists Tim Korychuck, Stephenie Walker, and Frank Norton, Jr. Ana Merino's poems, "Good-bye Childhood" and "Doodle the Genie" (translated from Spanish into English by Toshiya Kamei), respond to J. M. Barrie's play, *Peter Pan, or, the Boy Who Wouldn't Grow Up* (1904), as well as folktales about genies, such as those popularized in *The Arabian Nights Entertainment* (English edition, 1706). Similarly, Laura Lee Washburn responds to and reinterprets P. L. Travers' *Mary Poppins* (1934) in "The Right Answer" and the beleaguered and betrayed heroines of many European folktales in "A Story."

Again drawing for inspiration from William Blake, the "Songs of Experience" in Section Four include historically-themed images, poetry, and fiction by Jacek Fraczak, Burton Raffel, and Caleb True, focusing on the intersection of childhood and adolescence with violence and war, as well as contemporary coming-of-age poetry and fiction by Joe Cover, D. Gilson, Shiloh Peters, and Katlyn Minard.

Julie Blackmon is an internationally acclaimed photographer whose work is influenced by Seventeenth-Century Dutch and Flemish painters who provide "personal narratives of family life" to "explore the fantastic elements of ... everyday lives, both imagined and real." Her four photographs set the stage for Section Five, "Performing Childhood," which focuses on music, drama, and film for children. Jean Stringam has contributed two original songs "performed" by characters in two of her children's novels. "My Joke About a Worm" is a rap featuring Cheyenne and Joaquin, the young male protagonists of *The Hoarders* (2001), while "All I Want" is a personal expression of things that Adele, the narrator of *Balance* (2011), feels are important. Renée Dunn originally wrote "What to Say," a play intended for use in high school classrooms, in a course that Stringam taught in writing for children and young adults. In "Horror and the Horrible Child in Pixar's *Toy Story*," Ken Gillam and Shannon R. Wooden explore attitudes towards children and play in the so-called children's films produced by Pixar, particularly *Toy Story*, which treats various forms of play and performance by children.

The rich offerings from so many genres found here could not have come together without a collaborative effort from my co-editor, Linda Trinh Moser, the editors of Moon City Press, and the students involved in the reading and commenting on this work: Tim Leyrson, Laura Dimmit,

Matt Whitaker, Jessica Stogsdill, Heather Cook, Hilary Johnson, Mandi Reed, and Abby Hill. A very special thanks goes to Eric Pervukhin, who designed the interior and cover. This would have been much less of a volume without all of their efforts, and I am truly grateful.

Work Cited

Clark, Beverly Lyon. *Kiddie Lit: The Cultural Construction of Children's Literature*. Baltimore: Johns Hopkins UP, 2003. Print.

Teddybear by Kathryn Turner

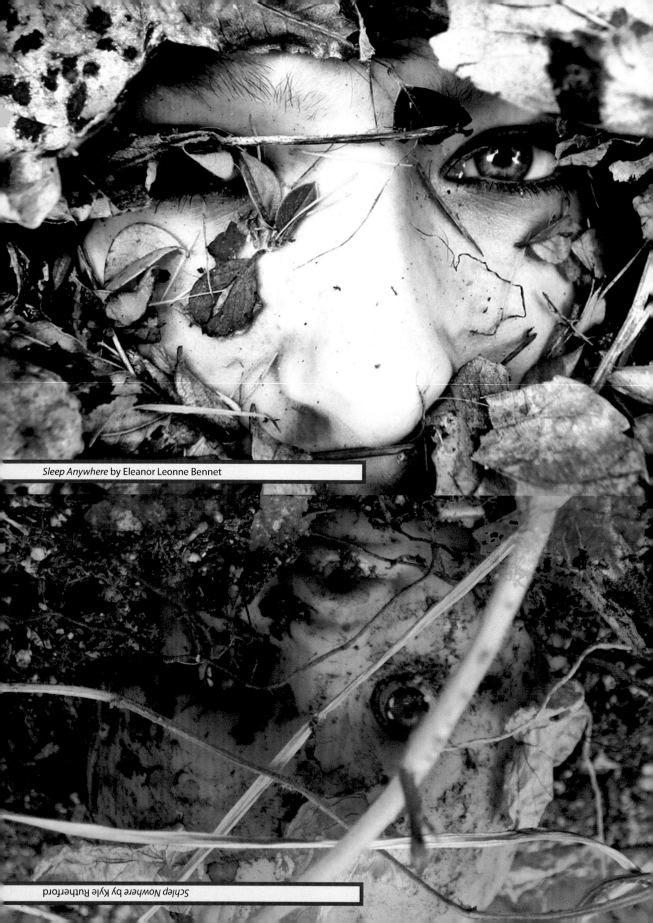

Sleep Anywhere by Eleanor Leonne Bennet

Schlep Nowhere by Kyle Rutherford

I. Songs of Innocence

Teddybear by Jeremy Kistler

David Harrison

That's When I Knew

She made me magic capes,
draped sheets on clotheslines
to form secret chambers
where superheroes met.
There we sat cross-legged,
muttered mysterious incantations,
swore solemn oaths
to rescue maidens.

Mere mortals never knew
that my quilt,
placed just so on summer days,
transformed into a rocket ship
or that on it I explored
the remotest regions of the universe,
vanquishing alien demons
too dangerous to describe.

Inside the cavernous,
twisting halls of my lair
beneath the table,
she served special cookies
so I could see through walls,
milk for my muscles of steel.
Thus fortified I fought off evil,

rescued maidens who dwelled within
the corridors of my mind.

I knew, then,
when I was six,
how to use my supernatural powers
to save the world.

David Chewed His Fingernails

David chewed his fingernails,
his dad said not to do it.
David tried but couldn't stop,
he'd grab a nail and chew it.

He chewed up all his fingernails
and said, "I'm sorry, Pop,
but I can reach my toenails, too,
and it's too late to stop."

He nibbled toenails one by one
and started on a toe.
"You'll ruin yourself," his father warned,
"The farther up you go."

David said, "I know it's bad,
but I can't break this habit."
He chewed
and chewed and chewed
and chewed,
nibbling like a rabbit.

 Father rolled his weary eyes,
"I told him so," he said.
Now all that's left of David are his
shoes
and teeth …
and
head.

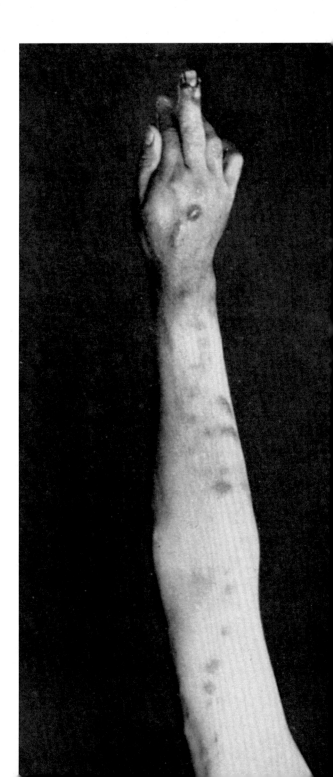

Donna Barkman

Elizabeth

This was Elizabeth's first trip to visit Great-Aunt Betsy. It was also her first time to travel all by herself. But it wasn't her first bus ride. She and Mom used to take the bus downtown on Sunday afternoons to see a puppet show or to window shop.

This time, Dad put her on a bus going out to the countryside and gave the driver her ticket. The driver smiled at her and then at her dad, who said, "Her name is Elizabeth. Keep an eye on her, please." He knew that the driver needed her other eye for driving.

Elizabeth sat in the front seat next to a boy who looked like a grown-up but seemed like a kid. She guessed he was a teenager. She could hear a little bit of the music sneaking out of his earphones. He nodded his head in time to the drumbeat. She wondered if she would act like that when she was a teenager.

The trip was zippy fast. Soon no more houses packed together with fences and hedges between. Soon no more stores in little strips. Soon came big grassy stretches and tall green plants with mermaid hair that Elizabeth guessed were rows of corn. There were barns and silver silos that Dad had told her were for storing grain for horses and pigs. "I'll ask Great-Aunt Betsy if he's right," thought Elizabeth. She was a toddler when she had last seen her great aunt, but they had often talked on the phone. Elizabeth loved Great-Aunt Betsy's booming voice and the strange and funny words she liked to use.

Before she knew it, they came into a town with a few saggy buildings. A hardware store, a general store, a small food shop with a post office sign on it. And with a bus stop sign on it, too! Elizabeth figured that they were there. Then she saw a tall woman in overalls and a baseball cap watching the bus come close and closer. She jumped from her seat and waved through the big front window. The driver said, her eye on Elizabeth, "Until we've come to a full stop, please stay in your seat." Quickly, Elizabeth sat on the edge of hers, still waving.

When the door opened with a big sighing noise, she looked at the driver, who smiled OK. Elizabeth scurried down the steps into Great-Aunt Betsy's hug. "How was your journey?" She used words like "journey" instead of "trip."

"Splendid," Elizabeth answered. That was another word Great-Aunt Betsy had taught her.

"My vehicle's right here," Great-Aunt Betsy boomed as she picked up Elizabeth's backpack and tossed it lightly into the back of her shiny little pickup truck. It landed on top of a big block of hay, or was it straw, Libby wondered.

"Let's get a move on," her aunt said. "No use lollygagging when there's not much to do in this little burg and there's plenty to do at home."

Elizabeth was curious about what Great-Aunt Betsy had in mind, but she felt a bit too shy to ask. She knew that her great aunt was a veterinarian—a big-animal vet. That meant she took care of horses and cows and pigs when they were sick or hurt. But she was retired now, so why was there plenty to do at home?

Great-Aunt Betsy opened the passenger door of her truck and Elizabeth pulled herself up onto the seat, thrilled to be riding in front for the first time. She would explain to her dad later that in this truck there was no back seat for kids. She was up so high that she felt like she could see

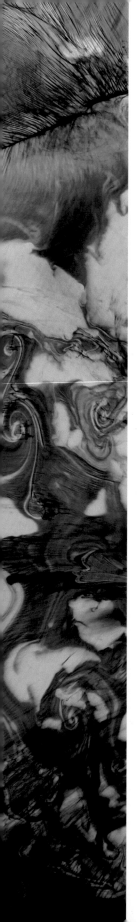

the whole world in front and on both sides, even with the seat belt holding her firmly in place.

Great-Aunt Betsy drove as carefully as if she had a crystal goblet on the seat beside her. First they were on paved streets. Then they bumped along over winding dirt roads. Elizabeth pointed to the tall green plants with mermaid hair. "You're right; that's corn," said Great-Aunt Betsy. "The tassels are called silk because that's what they feel like."

Elizabeth pointed to the silos. Great-Aunt Betsy said, "Your dad is right. They'll soon be full of grain, like corn and oats to feed the farmers' livestock in the winter."

Elizabeth pointed to the bundles in the back of the truck. "Is that hay or straw?" she asked. "And what's it for?"

Great Aunt Betsy answered, "It's straw." She smiled mysteriously. "And soon, you'll know what it's for." She drove on and on. Elizabeth was dumbfounded at how far and wide the farm fields went.

Finally, they came to a narrow lane. "One-way traffic here!" Great-Aunt Betsy laughed. "This is my own, my long, long driveway." She pulled up to a house that looked very small from the front. "Believe it or not, this part used to be a chicken coop," she roared. "It was a bit too small for people, so I added a room or two over the years."

Elizabeth was astounded to discover room after room, sometimes up a few steps, sometimes down. Every one of them was cozy and inviting. "Here's yours," said Great-Aunt Betsy, as she bowed Elizabeth through the door. "It's my special guest room, where your mother used to stay when she was a girl, a lot like you."

Elizabeth looked at the bed, piled high with pillows. She stared out the wide windows at the fields beyond, lined with rows of silken-tasseled corn. She noticed the pictures of animals on every wall and every flat surface—the desk and dresser and bedside table. There were paintings and sketches of horses, cows, sheep, pigs, dogs, cats, chickens, goats and … was that a unicorn embroidered on the cushion on the window seat?

24

Her mom loved all kinds of animals. Elizabeth tried to imagine her mother here in this very room. Then she spotted a photo of a girl in blue jeans and pigtails, one on either side of a huge grin. "Is that my mother?" she asked.

Great-Aunt Betsy was unusually quiet for a moment. "Yes, that's Libby, all right, way before she grew up and met your dad and had you. Way before she got sick."

Elizabeth took a deep breath, her gaze on her great aunt's face. "Do you think my mom will ever get well?"

"Have you talked with your dad about that?" asked Great-Aunt Betsy.

"I've tried. He just says he doesn't know, and then he looks so sad, I can't ask again."

Great-Aunt Betsy took Elizabeth's hands in hers and spoke quietly. "Your mother has a fiercely bad sickness and most people who have it don't ever get better."

Elizabeth stared at the photograph, pushing back tears so they trickled down her throat. Yet she was somehow happy to be in this room where her mother had slept many years ago. She cleared her throat, swallowed, and spoke a little gruffly. "Why did you call my mother Libby? Her name was Elizabeth, like mine."

"It was, indeed, Elizabeth, but we often called her Libby. My name is Elizabeth, too, but I'm called Betsy. Your grandmother was also Elizabeth! Do you remember calling her Grandma Betty? That was her nickname."

Elizabeth pondered the facts. "We all have different nicknames from the same exact name. Well, I'll be hornswoggled"—a word that made both of them smile. But Great-Aunt Betsy looked surprised. "You don't have a nickname. We always call you Elizabeth."

"Sometimes my Dad swings me around and around and then he says, "Lizzie, Lizzie, Bet You're Dizzy, so sometimes he calls me Dizzy Lizzie." With that, Elizabeth opened her backpack and started to put her clothes in the dresser.

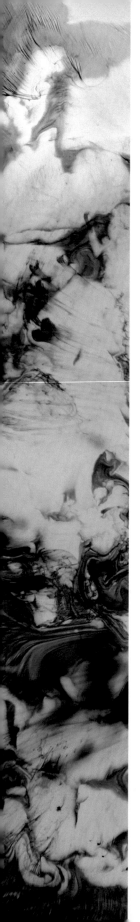

"Whoa," Great-Aunt Betsy interrupted. "First, let's have some lunch. I hope you're not a persnickety eater. Will peanut butter on homemade rye bread do?"

Elizabeth wasn't sure she liked rye bread, but she didn't want to be persnickety. After only one bite, she found it was delicious. Especially washed down with fresh lemonade. Later, as she wiped chocolate frosting off her chin from the cupcakes they'd had for dessert, Elizabeth was ready with two questions. "What is the straw for and what is the plenty-to-do that you mentioned?"

"Aha!" Great-Aunt Betsy responded. "The straw is part of our plenty-to-do. I'll leave these dishes soaking in the sink and you can come with me."

Elizabeth followed her great aunt from the kitchen through a big screened-in porch, out the back door, past a vegetable patch to a shed behind the garage. Great-Aunt Betsy gently opened the shed door. Elizabeth peered into the dim light and gasped. Inside was a huge golden dog lying on a folded blanket. The dog was panting quietly and her belly was bulging. "I'm flabbergasted," whispered Elizabeth. "Who is she and why is she here and when will she have her pups?" She and Great-Aunt Betsy were crouched in the doorway.

"Probably tonight or tomorrow, to answer your last question first," murmured her great aunt. "She's here because the animal shelter called and asked me to help out with a homeless dog. They found her roaming the streets. No collar, no tags. I don't know who she is. But I thought you could help with that. Find just the right name for her."

Great-Aunt Betsy straightened up quickly. "Let's get to work and spread that straw on the floor. Those pups will need some padding to rest and to play on. They'll be messy little rascals, too. When the straw gets soiled, we'll replace it with a fresh batch."

Elizabeth was amazed at how heavy the straw bales were. Together, she and Great-Aunt Betsy carried them, one at a time, to the shed. They stacked two in a corner and spread the straw from the third evenly on the floor, making a fragrant bed. The dog eyed them calmly. Great-Aunt

Betsy examined her with expert eyes and hands. "Those pups will be coming soon," she predicted. "I'll do the lunch dishes while you unpack. Then may be we can play a game or two of Crazy Eights before we check on her again."

The afternoon passed quietly and slowly. Elizabeth found it hard to concentrate on the game. "What's this, Miss Dizzie-Lizzie—you've lost three times in a row," teased Great-Aunt Betsy. "I didn't think you were a flibbertigibbet."

"I'm not," laughed Elizabeth. "I just have some things on my mind." She was thinking about her mother's picture and all the Elizabeths in her family. She was also composing a list of names for the beautiful big dog. Harriet? Clarissa? Genevieve? Nothing seemed right.

She was still deep in thought when Great-Aunt Betsy jumped up. "I think I hear something! Come!" They raced to the shed and slipped inside. Three small balls of fur squirmed on the floor while the mama dog licked them, one after another. When she noticed her visitors, a low growl warned them away.

"Hush, sweetie," whispered Great-Aunt Betsy. "I just want to see if your babies are OK." She gently checked each pup and the mother, handling them as if they were delicate flowers. Already some of the straw was soiled. She tossed it out while Elizabeth helped spread a clean dry layer.

"She'll get used to you soon, Elizabeth. And then you can handle the pups. Maybe in the morning."

Elizabeth could hardly sleep that night, waiting for the lazy sun to come up. At first light, she jumped into her clothes and ran to the kitchen where Great-Aunt Betsy was pouring orange juice into two glasses. "Down the hatch, Elizabeth! Let's skedaddle. The pups are awake."

They raced to the shed. Great-Aunt Betsy slowly opened the door. A bright sunbeam burst through, lighting the huge golden dog, lying on her side. The three pups were drinking her nourishing milk.

"They're gorgeous," sighed Elizabeth, "When they're done eating, may I touch them?"

"We'll let the mother decide that," answered her great aunt.

Elizabeth quietly approached the puppies. She listened for a growl from the mama. Not a sound. She picked up the smallest baby. "This one is a humdinger," she laughed. "This wiggly one is a skinnamarink, and this big one is a lollapalooza".

Great-Aunt Betsy was stroking the mother, keeping her calm. Then she looked at each pup closely. "They're all girls, Elizabeth. Have you decided on names besides humdinger, skinnamarink, and lollapalooza?" she teased.

Elizabeth nodded solemnly. "I want to call the mother Margaret. It's a dignified name for a brave dog. And I'd like to call her pups the nicknames for Margaret—Margie for the biggest one, Maggie for the middle one, and Peg for the little one. They'll all be Margarets, just like we are all Elizabeths."

"And you know what?" she continued. "If I ever have a little girl of my own, I'll name her Elizabeth, of course. And her nickname will be Beth."

"A splendid plan," agreed Great-Aunt Betsy. "And it saves all the rigamarole of trying to find another name. Beth, I mean Elizabeth, is perfect. Your mother will be pleased."

With that, Great-Aunt Betsy and Elizabeth bid a temporary good-bye to the dog and pups and headed into the house. It was time for breakfast and neither one was at all persnickety about what it would be.

Mandi Reed

Brian and the Great Button Chase

Brian made lots of messes with his baby brother just for fun, but his favorite thing to do was play video games.

Most of the time Brian's mother ran to and fro, to and fro. "Help me pick up laundry," she said.

But Brian looked for treasure instead.

"Help me peel potatoes," she said.

But Brian fought a pirate instead.

"Change your brother's diaper!" Mom said.

But Brian turned up his nose and played for high scores instead.

One day Brian saw a loose button on his controller. He pressed pause and—POP! The button jumped off the controller and rolled right under the front door.

"Oh no!" he said.

Brian chased the button. It disappeared under a door on the porch he had never seen before. Brian opened the door and tumbled into a great, dark hole!

Brian fell and fell and fell. He plopped onto the street of a new world. Spare parts littered the ground.

"Where am I? Where are all the people?"

"Little boy!" a voice called. "Stay where you are!"

Brian looked up. A Streetlight was talking to him.

"Have you seen my button?" Brian asked.

"It rolled down the road, but don't go looking for it! The robot that lives at the next corner will find you! He turns kids into spare parts for his inventions. He might even turn you into a Streetlight like me!"

"But I need to find my button!"

Brian ran to the next corner, where he found his button—right in the robot's hand!

"Psst!" another Streetlight said. "Hide!"

The robot came closer. Brian tried to squeeze in behind the light pole.

"Hello, Streetlight," said Robot. He reached around the pole and caught Brian's sleeve. "This boy must come with me."

"Don't turn him into spare parts!" said Streetlight.

"I might not," Robot said. "But he must clean up my messes. I'm running out of space to invent things."

Brian and Robot went into a building. They took the only elevator to the top floor. What a mess! After some time, Robot gave Brian a strange-looking watch. On it was Brian's lost button.

"Only push the middle button," Robot said. "It will pause time. Then you can do all my chores and still have time to play. But whatever you do, don't push any other buttons. Not even the one from your controller. Bad things will happen."

Brian was still a little afraid of being turned into spare parts, so he did just as Robot said.

Although he worried about the Streetlights, life was pleasant enough for a time. Then Brian began to miss his mother. He thought of how she always ran to and fro, to and fro. He wondered if the Streetlights missed their mothers, too.

Then one day, a strange thing happened. Brian accidentally pushed a forbidden button, and—WHOOSH! Some spare parts on the floor turned back into kids!

"Hey!" one boy said. "You did it! You turned us back with Robot's watch!"

Brian smiled, because he knew what to do. Soon all the spare parts in Robot's apartment were kids again.

"Everybody in the elevator," Brian whispered.

Robot looked up from his workbench just as the elevator doors closed. All his kids were escaping! He rolled to stop them, but he was too late.

Brian and the other children reached the street and tumbled out of the elevator. Brian held the elevator door open with one hand. With the other hand, he pushed the forbidden button on Robot's watch as fast as he could. He changed all the spare parts—and Streetlights—into kids again. Then he pushed the button from his video game controller. Hundreds of new doorways appeared.

Finally Brian pushed pause. He tossed the watch into the elevator. It froze in time, never to move again. Robot was stuck on the top floor!

"Got him!" Brian said.

The other kids cheered. Then everyone ran for a new door and went safely home again.

Brian romped around his room in delight—until he noticed his messes. He began to pick up his laundry.

"Why don't you look for treasure?" Mom said.

But Brian peeled potatoes instead.

"Want to fight a pirate?" Mom said.

But Brian changed his brother's diaper instead.

"I thought I needed to do your chores," Mom said.

But Brian had been helping, so the family played together instead.

Judith Gero John

Counsel for "Babees": Fathers, Mothers, and Early Advice Books for Children

From the medieval manner book *The Babees' Book* (ca. 1475)[1] to the more modern children's advice book, Judge Judy Sheindlin's *You Can't Judge a Book by Its Cover: Cool Rules for School* (2001), adults feel obligated to instruct. Parents especially want to help their children achieve "success"— whether that success is wealth, happiness, respect, or heaven. Mothers and fathers, however, often assume different roles in advising their children and speak to them in different voices. The differing nature of parental advice was established in the Sixteenth and Seventeenth Centuries, when advice books became especially popular because of the rise of the middle class, the changing nature of the family, and the early deaths of many parents, especially mothers.

From Boethius's *De Consolatione Philosophiae* (AD 523) to The Exeter Book (ca. 1046) to *The Dictes and Sayings of the Philosophers* (1477),[2] the English valued advice books, both published and private. The advice manuals by these early writers were the de facto textbooks of early schooling in Britain. The rise of the middle class, however, created a new demand for published advice books. There was an outpouring of books about raising and educating children. As the importance of children grew in middle-class culture, merchants, who were themselves becoming important to England's growth as an economic and world power, began paying special attention to the education of their children. The expansion of the middle class in both size and power had a profound effect on English culture, but nowhere was this more obvious than in printed books.

Louis B. Wright, in *Middle-Class Culture in Elizabethan England* (1935), sees the rise of the middle class as key in the development of advice books. He writes,

> The discovery of some Northwest Passage to learning, some short route to the information and culture demanded by the "complete citizen," was sought during the sixteenth and seventeenth centuries with a zeal that equaled that of the traders and voyagers who strove to find quicker passages to the material wealth of the Orient. Prosperous merchants, thrifty tradesmen, all that increasing multitude of citizens who made up a commercial class ambitious for advancement, were eager for self-improvement. While the Renaissance courtier perhaps cultivated the arts and graces that made him the accomplished personality described by a Castiglione or a Peacham, his cousin, the tradesman, was pursuing an ideal of education that multiplied his accomplishments and increased his stock of useful and cultural information. For the Renaissance spirit was confined to no class, however different its manifestations might be in different groups.
>
> Since, however, the citizen had less time and means than the courtier for attaining his ends, he required speedy methods of instruction and usable compendiums of facts. The answer to his demands was the handbook, the printed guide, the Tudor and Stuart counterpart of the modern fifteen-easy-lessons which led to bourgeois perfection. (121)

One quick way for the middle-class merchant to raise his status was to marry a son or daughter to the child of a nobleman. While the noble eldest son, who by law of primogeniture inherited all, might not be interested in marrying beneath his station, younger sons would be happy to have a bride whose family could support him in the style to which he had become accustomed. Noble daughters found marriage to a middle-class

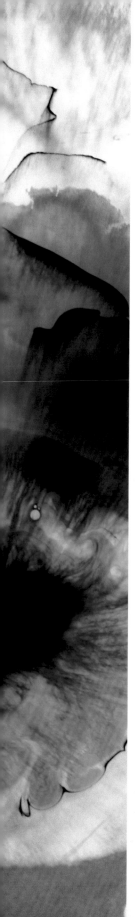

man an escape from the convent life forced upon many aristocratic ladies. However, while many among the middle class were looking to become upwardly mobile, others were concerned with their children's happiness and salvation in the next world. These concerns are part of the impetus for the eventual publication of so many private diaries and letters as advice books.

A new interest in children also arose because of the changing nature of the family. Most medieval families were extended families, including brothers, sisters, uncles, grandparents, and children, all living together. During this time it was the norm for children to be entailed (sent to other homes to be educated as squires, cupbearers, etc.) as early as age seven or eight. However, with the introduction of humanist philosophy, the notion of a divine hierarchy (God, King, Father, Mother, Child), and the cultural ascent of Protestantism, the nuclear family evolved and developed throughout England. Parents began to take to heart their responsibility for the moral upbringing of their children. The emergence of Protestantism has often been credited with a greater interest in educating children, but many other factors encouraged parents to pay more attention to their children.[3] Again, as social roles changed and people had to redefine themselves, they desired printed guides to help them understand and define these roles.

For centuries in England (and still in some countries today), the announcement of a pregnancy came with a probable death sentence. And while death through childbirth was strictly a female fear, men also knew life was short. Children often did not survive birth or childhood; those who did could not count on their parents living to see them reach adulthood. Death, the great leveler, haunted the lives of rich and poor, Catholic and Protestant, children and adults, men and women. Looking into the face of death gave most men and women of this time the urge to write advice to their children. Few wrote with an eye to publication, although most of the books that have endured were eventually published. The writings are the thoughts, fears, and hopes of parents who might not

34

live to see their children grow up. Many quoted popular teachings or maxims of the time, but their works are also full of personal observations, poems, stories, and prayers.

Both fathers and mothers feared early deaths, and most were well-founded fears. John "Mathew" Rogers, a Protestant martyr, was burned at the stake in front of his wife and children. Rogers's final writings were penned to his children while he was awaiting execution for heresy during the reign of Mary, and these were published in 1557 as the work of a Protestant martyr.[4] Rogers expresses a view typical of the Protestant parent of his time: this world is a vale of tears and the only hope in life is to avoid sin.

In 1598, James VI of Scotland (later James I of England) wrote *Basilikon Doron* for his infant son, Prince Henry.[5] James was concerned about his own health and took seriously his roles as patriarch of his country and primary teacher of his son, the future king. As king, he was aware that his private thoughts could not be separated from his public persona, although he never considered publishing the book and commissioned the creation of only seven copies. While he writes for his child, he is aware that others may read his words. He shows his dual concern in the salutation to his introduction: "To Henrie My Dearest Sonne and Natural Successour" (A1). His introductory remarks spell out his understanding of his role as father and king:

> Whome to can so rightly appertein this booke, of the Institution
> of a Prince in all the poyntes of his calling, as well generall (as
> a Christian towardes God) as particuler (as a King towardes his
> people?) whome to (I say) can do it so justlie apperteine, as unto
> you my dearest Sonne? Since I the author thereof as your naturall
> Father, must be carefull for your godlie and vertuous education
> as my eldest Sonne, and the first fruites of Gods blessing towards
> me in my posteritie: And (as a King) must timouslie provide for
> your training up in all the poyntes of a Kinges office (since ye are

35

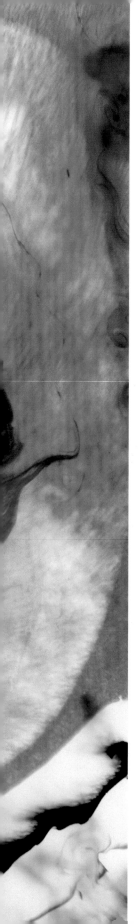

my naturall and lawfull Successour therein) that (being rightly informed hereby of the weight of your burthen) yee may in time begin to consider, that being borne to be a King, ye are rather borne to Onus, then Honos. (A1)

The king organizes the book into three parts:

> The first teacheth you your duty towards God as a Christian: the next your dutie in your office as a King: And the third teacheth you how to behave yourself in indifferent things, which of them-selves are neither right nor wrong, but according as they are rightly or wrongly used: & yet wil serve (according to your be-haviour therin) to augment or impair your fame and authoritie at the hands of your people. (A1)

The first section is twenty-three pages long and recommends that Henry refer to Scriptures in all matters of religion. He quotes extensively from both the New and the Old Testament, discussing how even the laws of governing might be traced to the Bible. He tells his son to "Keepe God sparinglie in your mouth, but aboundantlie in your hart" (E1).

The second part, dealing with the duties of the king, is ninety-four pages long and deals primarily with the "establishing, and executing [of] good lawes" (E2). This includes advice for dealing with Parliament and with traitors, as well as covering problems associated with doling out justice. Other subjects include the minting of coins, the association be-tween church and state, the relationship between a king and his subjects, and the nature of the people with whom he should surround himself at the court. The subject of marriage also falls under the section of kingly responsibilities, rather than personal ones. Although this section concen-trates on the personal obligations and choices concerning marriage, there is always the implication that the marriage of a king affects his subjects, especially through the birth of a successor.

36

The final thirty-nine pages, dealing with "indifferent things," are concerned with appearances. Although he avoids a Machiavellian approach, James warns his son that some of his subjects will judge him by his behavior. He writes, "The whole indifferent actiones of a man, I devide in two sortes: In his behaviour in thinges necessarie, as foode, sleeping, raymente, speaking, writing, and gesture: And in thinges not necessarie (though conveniente and lawfull) as pastimes or exercises, and using of companie for recreation" (R2). This section is an odd combination of social conventions—"Let your Table bee honorably served" (R2)—and concern regarding moral infractions—"but serve your appetite with few dishes (as young Cyurs did) which both is holesomest and freest from the vice of delicacie, which is a degree of glutonie" (R2-R3). The book encompasses most of the varied kinds of advice available during this period, including counsel on manners, sports, and avoiding the seven deadly sins. Although there is an obvious and emphatic concern for moral issues, even the king recognizes that men are frequently judged by outward appearances and must attend to the practical affairs of state. Here is a father, and a king, who sees himself as father of his people, speaking his mind about all matters of the world.

Sir Walter Raleigh was concerned with very practical matters when he wrote his "Instructions to His Son" while he was in the Tower of London under a death sentence.[6] Raleigh's work moves away from the strictly spiritual aspect of teaching a child and emphasizes necessary social and economic advice. Although it reflects a movement in the world from spiritual values to materialistic ones, it also reflects the fact that fathers may be more aware of the practical needs of their children than mothers appear to be. Sir Walter, in the Tower, must have certainly been aware that political, social, and economic acumen would help his child as much as, if not more than, religious instruction. He seems to care not only for the soul of his son, but also for the quality of his life. He is able to call upon his own experiences to support his advice. He begins his first chapter,

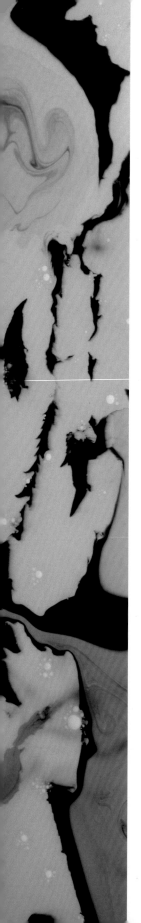

There is nothing more becoming a wise man than to make choice of friends, for by them thou shalt be judged what thou are. Let them, therefore, be wise and virtuous and none of those that follow thee for gain. But make election rather of thy betters than thy inferiors, shunning always such as are poor and needy, for if thou givest twenty gifts and refuse to do the like but once, all that thou hast done will be lost and such men will become thy mortal enemies. (Wright, *Advice* 19)

This could well be a comment on Raleigh's own life as easily as it is advice to his son, and although his advice borrows from conventional wisdom, coming from Raleigh in prison, it certainly takes on the authority of one whose experiences bear out the truth of what is said.

Elizabeth Grymeston's book, *Miscelanea, Meditations, Memoratives,* (1604), was the first mother's advice book published in England. She wrote her advice book to her son Bernye in 1603, the same year she died. Although it is impossible to know how long it took her to write it, it was not published until after her death. Grymeston begins a tradition of apologizing for writing which remains a part of women's writing into the Nineteenth Century. She feels compelled to write for a number of reasons: the force of a mother's love, the concern that her husband might not live to provide the proper upbringing, and her own belief that she was now "a dead woman among the living" (A3). She is moved by her own piety and concern to use the experience of her illness and impending death to gain the authority to speak. Using Scriptures, personal meditations, prayers, and a variety of stories and authors, she breaks "the barren soile of [her] fruitlesse braine" in order to leave her son a "counseller" in her absence (A3). However, her concern does not show an interest in publication, but rather an acceptance of the creed of the "silent, obedient wife." She is not writing for the world, and there is no combination of practical and economical advice to be found in this book.

38

Grymeston's concern for her son's spiritual salvation is obvious from the start. Her chapter titles include:

1. A Short line how to levell your life; 2. A mortified mans melancholie; 3. A patheticall speech in the person of Dives in the torments of hell; 4. Who lives most honestly will die most willingly; 5. A sinner's Glass; 6. The union of Mercie and Justice; 7. No greater crosse than to live without a crosse; 8. The feare to die, is the effect of an evill life; 9. That affliction is the coat of a true Christian; 10. A theme to thinke on; 11. Morning meditation, with sixteen sobs of a sorrowful spirit; 12. A Madregall; 13. Evening meditation; 14. Memoratives. (A2)

Grymeston recommends the importance of prayer:

When thou risest, let thy thoughts ascend, that grace may descend, and if thou canst not weepe for thy sinnes, then weepe, because thou canst not weepe.

Remember that Prayer is the wing wherewith thy soule flieth to heaven; and Meditation the eye wherewith we see God. …

Let thy sacrifice be an innocent heart: offer it dayly at set houres, with That devotion that well it may shew, that thou both knowest and acknowledgest his greatnesse before whom thou art. So carrie thy selfe as woorthie of his presence. (B2)

She barely touches on economic or social matters that often filtered into male advice of the time, but when she does, it is with an eye towards avoiding the occasion of sin:

Where thou owest, pay duetie: where thou findest, returne curtesie: where thou art knowen, deserve love. Desire the best: disdaine none, but evill companie. Grieve, but be not angry at

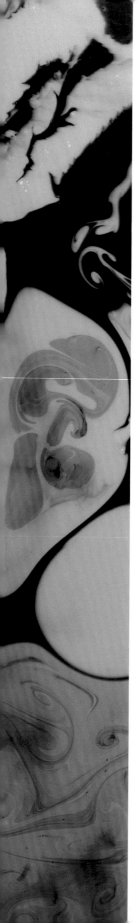

discourtesies. Redresse, but revenge no wrongs. Yet so remember pitie, as you forget not decencie. Let your attire be such, as may satisfie a curious eye; and yet beare witnesse of a sober minde. Arme your selfe with that modestie, that may silence that untemperate tongue, and control that unchaste eye, that shall aime at passion. (B2)

Grymeston's primary concern throughout the book is the spiritual salvation and enlightenment of her son. She discusses the nobility of the soul, the dangers of being trapped by the vanities of this life, the horrors of hell, and the salvation that follows a good death.

She concentrates on her subject with a diligence (she writes fourteen chapters—more than fifty pages) unmatched by patriarchal advice-givers (e.g., William Cecil,[7] Walter Raleigh, or Mathew Rogers). She is intent on saving her son's soul and calls upon all of her writing skills, the words of others, the power of prayer, and Scripture in order to reinforce advice which, though it does not stray from what fathers have asserted in earlier books, is more fervent. Rather than let herself drift to earthly matters—as Cecil and Raleigh do—or offer spiritual advice that can hardly be followed—as Rogers does—she concentrates on ways in which daily life might lead her son to sin. While some of her advice is in the form of platitudes, she brings all of it back to her son's relationship with God:

Be mindfull of things past; Carefull of things present; Provident of things to come. Goe as you would be met. [Seek] as you would be found. Speake as you would be heard: And when you goe to bed, read over the carriage of your selfe that day. Reforme that is amisse; and give God thanks for that which is orderly: and so commit thy selfe to him that keepes thee. (B2)

But whether she chooses examples from her own prayer life or copies prayers and psalms from prayer books and Scriptures, Grymeston's plan

40

is to provide a guide for her child. The decision to publish came after her death.

Elizabeth Jocelin's book, *The Mothers Legacie to Her Unborn Childe,* was written in 1621 (the same year as her death) and not published until 1624. She begins by letting her child know that she does not wish to teach those things that will gain earthly treasure; rather, she writes in the hope of setting the child on the path towards heaven. Like Grymeston, Jocelin also struggles with her own mortality. She writes to her husband in the prefatory letter:

> Mine own deare love, I no sooner conceived an hope, that I should bee made a mother by thee, but with it entred the consideration of a mothers duty, and shortly after followed the apprehension of danger that might prevent mee from executing that care I so exceedingly desired, I meane in religious training our Childe. And in truth death appearing in this shape, was doubly terrible unto mee. First, in respect of the painfulnesse of that kinde of death, and next of the losse my little one should have in wanting me.
>
> But I thanke God, these feares were cured with the remembrance that all things worke together for the best to those that love God, and a certaine assurance that hee will give me patience according to my paine. (A11-A12)

The threat of death due to pregnancy was uniquely a woman's experience, one shared only by mothers. Jocelin uses this experience to amplify her own voice, gaining authority from an experience which even her husband could not share.[8] Jocelin moves a step further by using the experience to gain a voice in the future of the child whose birth would signal her death.

Like others, Jocelin also recommends prayer, not because of convention but because of her own faith in God. Quoting Ecclesiastes 12:1, she

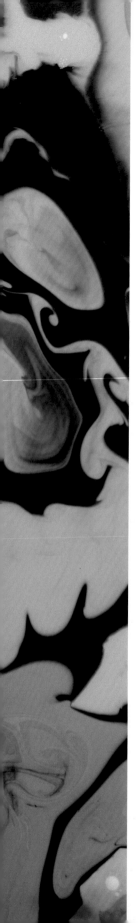

writes, "Remember thy Creator in the dayes of thy youth" (12). She asks her child to meditate on the benefits provided by the Creator: creation, sanctifying grace, and God's mercy. She recommends, as so many others have, morning meditation and prayer. However, she instructs the child to meditate on his or her sins first and then pray when fully awake. She then reviews the dangers of the seven deadly sins and the prayers that should be invoked in order to avoid them. In more mundane matters, such as dress, she writes:

> Mistake me not, nor give your selfe leave to take too much liber-
> ty with saying, My mother was too strict. No I am not, for I give
> you leave to follow modest fashion, but not to be a beginner of
> fashions: nor would I have you follow it till it be generall; so that
> in not doing as others doe, you might appear more singular than
> wise: but in one word, this is all I desire that you will not let your
> heart on such fooleries, and you shall see that this modest car-
> riage will win you reputation and love with the wise and vertuous
> sort. (35-36)

Jocelin continues by warning against pride, urging public prayer, and extolling the joy of receiving afflictions from God (based on the concept that God only sends crosses to those He loves). She calls upon other authorities less often than Grymeston, referring more often to her own belief (as in matters of dress). However, her attitude—that the salvation of the soul is the primary reason for existence—seems to be the same.

Dorothy Leigh's *The Mother's Blessing* (1616) uses the conventions of earlier advice books to create one of the most successful "handmade" publications of her time. Ostensibly written to her children while she was on her deathbed,[9] its subsequent published version "ran to fifteen editions between 1616 and 1630" (Beilin 275) and consists of 271 pages, not including thirteen pages of prefatory matter. The number of editions, as well as the length, is highly unusual for the time. Addressing her three

42

sons, Leigh initially focuses much of the early part of her book on why she writes. An apology and explanation is first found in her dedication to Princess Elizabeth: "Most worthy and renowned Princesse, I being troubled and wearied with feare, lest my children should not finde the right way to Heaven, thought with my selfe that I could do no lesse for them, then every man will doe for his friend, which was to write them the right way" (A2). In this example, Leigh does intend to publish her book and has acquired enough expertise concerning the world of printing to know to address her book to a sympathetic and powerful woman. She also claims her right to act as a man in the protection of her children's souls. Her book includes a letter of explanation to her sons, both apologizing and explaining her reasons for writing. She writes,

> My Children, God having taken your Father out of this vale of teares, to his Everlasting mercie in Christ, my selfe not onely knowing what a care hee had in his life time, that you should bee brought up godlily, but also at his death beeing charged in his Will, by the love and dutie which I bare him, to see you well instructed and brought up in knowledge, I could not choose but desire (according as I was also bound) to fulfill his will in all things, desiring no greater comfort in the world, then to see you grow in godlinesse, that so you might meets [sic] your father in Heaven, where I am sure he is, my selfe being a witnesse of his faith in Christ. And seeing my selfe going out of the world, and you but coming in, I know not how to perform this dutie so well as to leave you these few lines, which will shew you as well the great desire your Father had, both of your spirituall and temporall good, as the care I had to fulfill his will in this; knowing it was the last duty I should performe unto him. (A3)

Leigh includes several reasons why she writes in her opening poem, "Counsell to my Children," and her chapters begin with "causes" for

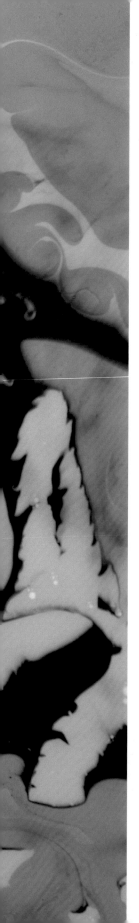

writing the book. She brilliantly uses the "law" of her husband's legal Will and Testament to circumvent the patriarchal "law" of the silent woman. She takes her obligation seriously enough to give a great deal of thought, not just to the content of her advice, but also to her presentation and her dedication. Leigh is apparently more comfortable writing than either of the other mothers discussed here, but she also shows that she has both the knowledge and the experience necessary to offer advice in a public manner, the printed book.

A Mother's Blessing consists of forty-five chapters; several offer explanations for the writing of the book, which alternate between public and private voice. Sometimes Leigh addresses her children personally ("the first cause of writing, is a motherly affection"), and at times she addresses a wider audience ("the third cause is, to move women to bee carefull of their children") (A4). She is obviously concerned with public reaction to her writing and is more self-conscious than either Grymeston or Jocelin. In addition to discussing the appropriateness of writing the book, Leigh includes a chapter on not fearing death, several chapters on the need for private prayer, and a chapter on the dangers of temptation. Leigh also quotes the Bible extensively, showing her knowledge of Scripture and adding emphasis to her own thoughts: "Is[aia]h 6.27: Labour not for the meat that perisheth, but for the meat that endureth to everlasting life" (7). Leigh is more concerned than either Grymeston or Jocelin with earthly matters, including the choice of wives, the naming of children, matters of dress, and the treatment of servants, but she never loses sight of how these things affect a child's relationship with God. She is one of the first women of her time to take what began as a "handmade" genre and turn it into a profitable publication.

Men and women both feel the need to advise their children, and whether dying or living, they hope their children hear what they have to say. In the Eighteenth and Nineteenth Centuries, with a clearer division between male and female roles, men grew more and more concerned with their public lives and their public voice, while many women were

44

satisfied to be the angels of the home and caretakers of the future by instilling morals and values in their children, sometimes in person and sometimes in their letters, diaries, and advice books. Most early advice books exist today because trunks of old papers once forgotten have been rediscovered, but more specifically because publishers and writers have discovered that personal advice made public can be profitable.

Notes

I have retained the spelling used in the editions of the sources cited throughout.

[1] Although this collection of advice concerning the waiting of tables and other manners was published in 1868, the actual advice comes from medieval sources.

[2] The first printed copy in England of *The Dictes and Sayings of the Philosophers* appeared in 1477.

[3] Protestants, especially Puritans, were extremely concerned about the child being born with mortal sin. Taking their roles as parents extremely seriously led them to both terrorize and torture their children in order to cure them of their wickedness. Books such as John Foxe's *Book of Martyrs* (1563), which recorded the deaths of many Protestant martyrs (including that of John "Mathew" Rogers), and which, according to Bingham and Scholt became required reading for all Protestant children in England and America, and later James Janeway's *Token for Children: Being an Exact Account of the Conversion, Holy and Exemplary Lives and Joyful Deaths of Several Young Children* (1671), emphasize the horrible method of intimidation used to make children follow the path of righteousness.

[4] I retain the name of Mathew Rogers to save confusion. Pollard and Redgrave assert that this was written by John Rogers, who had published some Protestant tracts under the pseudonym Thomas Matthews. Robert Smith, the publisher of their book, simply confused the two names when compiling some Protestant writings.

[5] Robert Waldegrave, printer to the king, also brought out an edition of James's *The True Lawe of Free Monarchies* in 1598. Although this is not, strictly speaking, an advice book written by a father to his son, *The True Lawe of Free Monarchies* is a parental advice book reflecting the view that the monarch is a parent to all of his subjects. In spite of James's concern for his own health, it was Henry who did not live to become king.

[6] Although Raleigh was executed in 1618, Wright shows that Raleigh's "Instructions" were first published in 1632 (Wright, *Advice* xix).

[7] William Cecil, Lord Burghley, wrote advice pamphlets for both of his sons and goes beyond Rogers by responding to the particular needs of his children. In 1561, he wrote "A Memorial for Thomas Cecil," and in 1584 he wrote "Certain Precepts for the Well Ordering of a Man's Life" for his son Robert (Wright, *Advice*).

[8] Although there were a few male midwives and plenty of advice books from the medical profession, bearing children was still a predominantly female concern even during the Renaissance, and women could use this shared experience to gain authority within their own groups.

[9] Dorothy Leigh is not listed in the *DNB* so it is difficult to verify the date of her death or whether she was dying when she wrote her book.

Works Cited

Al-Mubashshir ibn Fatik, Abu al-Wafa. AD 1000. *The Dictes and Sayings of the Philosophers. A Facsimile Reproduction of the First Book Printed in England by William Caxton, in 1477*. London: Diploma, 1974. Print.

The Babee's Book: Medival Manners for the Young, Done Into Modern English from Dr. Furnivall's Text by Edith Rickert. Trans. Edith Rickert. New York: Cooper Square, 1966. Print.

Beilin, Elaine. *Redeeming Eve: Women Writers of the English Renaissance*. Princeton: Princeton UP, 1987. Print.

Bingham, Jane, and Grayce Scholt. *Fifteen Centuries of Children's Literature: An*

Annotated Chronology of British and American Works in Historical Context.
Westport, CT: Greenwood, 1980. Print.

Boethius, Anicius Manlius Severinus. *The Consolation of Philosophy.* AD 523.
Trans. I. T. Ed. William Anderson. London: Centaur, 1963. Print.

Castiglione, Baldassare. *The Book of the Courtier.* New York: Penguin, 1967. Print.

Foxe, John. "Actes and Monuments." *Foxes Book of martyrs: a history of the lives,
sufferings, and triumphant deaths of the early Christian and the Protestant martyrs.* c. 1563. Ed. William Byron Forbush. Grand Rapids: Zondervan, 1978. Print.

Grymeston, Elizabeth. *Miscelanea, Meditations, Memoratives.* 1604. Early English Books 1475-1640. Reel 1048 [Microfilm].

James I. *Basilikon Doron.* 1599. Menston, UK: Scholar, 1969. Print.

Janeway, James. *Token for Children: being an exact Account of the Conversion,
holy and exemplary Lives and Joyful Deaths of several young Children.* c. 1671.
London: Dorman Newman, 1676. Print.

Jocelin, Elizabeth. *The Mothers legacie, to her unborne Childe.* 2nd impression.
1624. Early English Books 1475-1640. Reel 558 [Microfilm].

Krapp, George Philip and Elliott Van Kirk Dobie, eds. *The Exeter Book.* Morn-
ingside Heights, NY: Columbia UP, 1936. Print.

Leigh, Dorothy. *The Mother's Blessing: or, The Godly Counsaile of a Gentle-wom-
an, not long since deceased, left behind her for her children.* 10th ed. 1627. Early
English Books 1475-1640. Reel 805 [Microfilm].

Pollard, A. W., and G. R. Redgrave. *A Short Title Catalogue of Books Printed in
England, Scotland & Ireland and of English Books Printed Abroad, 1475-1640.*
London: The Bibliographic Society, 1948. Print.

Rogers, John (a.k.a. Thomas Matthew). *An exhortation of Mathew Rogers unto
his Children.* 1559. Early English Books 1475-1640. Reel 238 [microfilm].

Sheindlin, Judy. *Judge Judy Sheindlin's You Can't Judge a Book By Its Cover: Cool
Rules for School.* Illus. Bob Tore. New York: Cliff Street, 2001. Print.

Wright, Louis B. *Middle-Class Culture in Elizabethan England.* Chapel Hill: U of
North Carolina P, 1935. Print.

Wright, Louis B., ed. *Advice to A Son: Precepts of Lord Burghley, Sir Walter Raleigh, and Francis Osborne.* Ithaca, NY: Cornell UP, 1962. Print.

Teddybear by Sara Spoering

II. Beasts and Fabulous Creatures

G is for *Gaining*,
as every Child could;
A half pound a Month
is the least that he should.

wd.

Julie Platt

Abecedarius for a Child

Alpha Centauri was the first man born of horse. He brags about you to
     the sky using
ballistic missiles. *Run away, hold your ears.* On other days don't concern
     yourself; think about
Calliope, whom I've never seen. What color are her skirts, her stockings?
     How would she
decoupage her piano: with newspapers, leaves, or the thin skins of
     grapes?
Elephantitis is pitiable; cluck your tongue. But when you get beneath the
     branches, inside your secret
fable-place, leer and look and leer at the growth in your mind, the
     possibility that
ginger is harvested from these. Jonah and Ahab went walking
     without
harpoons; Nero sulked behind. Remember friendship begins with the
     exclusion of sharp edges.
Isolation tanks are something else entirely; you go there to divide. If
     you see
Jabberwocky, remember that he is your uncle. On the lilac trees, he can
     reach the tallest blooms.
Kore scrubbed and swept the locust husks from all the cornfields every
     Sunday so that
Leonardo da Vinci could measure a single cog in his flying machine. If
     you must go to
Mongolia, do not bring a camera. Drink goat's milk, walk barefoot,
     record only what you think

Neruda might be proud to hear. When you go to school, close your eyes.
	Speak only
ornithology and French to those who share your lunch table. Your
		mother is much more than a
pleasure principle; she is the murderer and the murdered, and she
		is God.
Queer is your currency. Do not waste a cent. If anyone asks, you should
		tell them that
Rosencrantz and Guildenstern are not, in fact, dead. Fire in the West is
		represented by the
salamander. There is no fire in the East; they chop wood, they carry
		water, they speak
Tagalog, which those around you will understand to be a kind of fruit.
	Wear dirty
underwear in case you are not in an accident; then, you will not have to
		change your life.
Violet is most beautiful when you are young and your mouth can
		cushion the drop of the o.
Warsaw is a good place to study the archived dance cards of angels and of
		devils. The
xylem is the marrow of the sunflower. The stars are the white blood cells
		that emerge.
Yellow is the color of your true love's belly if black is the color of his hair.
	Tira lira is the
zeitgeist for the world that has forgotten Lancelot, but you must recall
		how to cite him.

T is a *Topic*
which *Trouble* begins;
Both *Tea* and Coffee
for Children are Sins.

W is for *Whiskey*,
the best thing to drink
Between Meals
as often as ever we think.

Nursery Rhyme for a Villain's Funeral

Spindle and sextant, cork and wire.
Little suits. Dreams with teeth.
Animal stumps. Fingertip flies.
Shoot the moon, unfasten the wreath.
Under bayberry arbors dividing the spoils.
New businesses, new phantoms to perplex.
Burning brush. Old flag, prepare the soil.
Bear the bunting. Unravel the hex.

Zombie Hustle

Am I of my tribe? All night, I've heard the others thirst
and merge. I found my heart at the outskirts of your return.
Are my eyes with you? Why won't you put them in? Stop
and be me for a spell. Tell me, how did this thirst for you
emerge? Share your needles, dear. Give me your vivid toes
and let our thirsts converge. Who will I be? Tough wires backstitch
this brain as if it's cursed with the clotted undersides of love,
the disremembered un-urge. Grab hold of my jaw and clamp
it closed. Pity this hopping corpse! This apoptotic pup, nursing
at the verge, up against your window! I'm redoubling the taboo,
re-setting the table. Troubled? You're half in me. Want you back?
Between the panes we break like a thirst, like lovers into sweat,
like laws that govern halves of worms. Want you then the head? The bed?

I is for *Iron*
in Spinach and Eggs,
Builds Red Blood and Sinews
for beautiful Legs.

David Harrison

A Hungry Fox

A hungry fox sat in a field
and licked his furry chin.
"I think for breakfast," said the fox,
"I'll catch a plumpy hen."

"If I can't have a hen," said he,
"I'll take a goose to munch.
A plumpy hen or juicy goose
would make a perfect lunch."

"If I can't have a hen or goose
to keep from growing thinner,
I'll take a waddly, quacky duck
to gobble for my dinner."

Alas, he saw no plumpy hen,
no juicy goose or duck,
and so he settled for a bug
and sobbed, "Oh darn my luck!"

The Feisty Pig of France

The feisty pig of France is prone to root
in search of buried fungus called the truffle.
The problem is he likes to eat the loot.

Farmer tries to train the spry galoot
to snout the fungus out by sniff and snuffle.
The feisty pig of France is prone to root.

Farmer can't control the greedy brute.
The pig will dig and fill a gallon duffel.
The problem is he likes to eat the loot.

When farmer yells, he doesn't give a hoot.
He swings his derriere in a shuffle.
The feisty pig of France is prone to root.

Sometimes the farmer prods him with a boot,
But swine hide is much too tough to ruffle.
The problem is he likes to eat the loot.

The pig is much too valuable to shoot
and farmer knows he'd lose if they should scuffle.
The feisty pig of France is prone to root.
The problem is he likes to eat the loot.

Once Upon a Time

100 million years ago,
give or take a few—
when dinosaurs ran around
stamping and screaming
and scaring small mammals—
there lived a wasp with a sweet tooth,
which is to say the wasp
preferred sugar water
to more traditional diets
of spider juice and grub goo.

What caused this curiously altered taste
is a mystery. One can't chalk it up
to good judgment, considering a brain
the size of this period.

Call it signs of the time:
time for blooming angiosperms,
time for bees,
time they got together.
The obliging wasp and its progeny
eventually produced a bee.

A little bit wasp but mostly bee,
the nectar lover got busy
sucking sweets and impregnating
coquettish blossomy plants
by wallowing in their sticky seeds
and spreading them around.

60

Tsunamis of pollen-bearing,
insect-toting plants covered the land.
Some have said the dinosaurs,
strangers to hay fever,
developed allergies that left them
vulnerable as sitting ducks
(to borrow a figure of speech from a cousin)
and ill-prepared for catastrophes lurking
on future horizons.

This probably never happened,
hay fever I mean,
but you have to admit
that a sneezing T-Rex—
a toothy island stranded amidst
a relentless sea of blossoms
while serious bees buzzed its head—
would be something.

And who among those first men,
tens of millions of years hence,
would have risked a finger
under T's twitching nostrils
to utter an approximated "gesundheit"?

When I see a bee,
sometimes I wonder if its ancestors—
still carrying carnivorous wasp-lust
in their genes—
took on the big guys armed with
the latest technology,
and won.

Morning News

Dusk has barely enough time to hide the day crew before full dark summons the night shift.

Toothy yawns and yearning bellies greet another evening of chance. At one time or another I've met all the players: foxes sniffing for hidden ducklings; skunk families strolling my yard, raccoons that should be arrested for repeatedly breaking into my attic; light-blinded opossums who lose lopsided duels with cars. Deer … coyotes … stray cats … they've all appeared on the hooded stage between my back door and the lake.

Their visits are rarely marked. Only snow gives them a slate on which to write their dramas. Even then they tell no more than they must.

Morning snow lies
zippered with clues
for mystery readers.

Did night spirits
nod mall-walker greetings—
    "Evening, Opossum."
    "Evening, Skunk." —
or conceal sly agendas?

What creature crouched
outside my door,
savoring hints from within
of lasagna scraps
and chocolate?

Here, Big-Tracks lunges after
Small-Tracks, their encounter
scuffling the snow. Here,
Big-Tracks drags its trophy,
smoothing a path rabbit-wide.

Hooves like Valentines cut in half
examine my pool,
unsafely tempted by day.

Nimble paws gain my planter,
leap down, turn the corner;
birdless feathers
tent like pick-up sticks
beneath my feeder.

I read quickly.
Today's wind soon sweeps
old stories out of print.

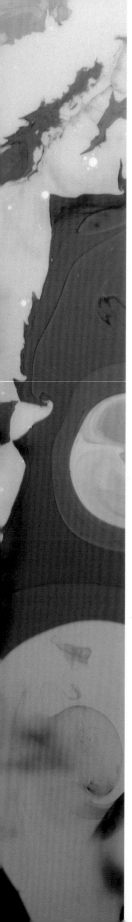

Chad Woody

The Honest Trout

Most of the fish in the Mississippi River were jerks and liars, but there was one good ol' trout who enjoyed nothing more than the telling of solid facts. Nobody paid much attention to him, because his statements were a little bit boring.

One time a barge full of beans was hit by a lightning bolt. All the fish were out bragging about themselves: how they were not scared of the lightning, how it baked the beans instantly, how they lit their cigarettes off the hot barge (even though everyone knows fish don't smoke), and how the thunder knocked them into the air where they did tricks.

"I did sixteen flips and ate a dragonfly before coming back down," said a catfish.

"I did a one-eighty and a three-sixty, and then I took a bite out of a cloud," said the bass.

"I got sucked through a jet engine and my heart stopped," said the walleye, "but the smell of all them beans cookin' got me going again! I ate at least four hundred!"

"I ate only one bean," recounted the honest trout. "It tasted burned but I went ahead and swallowed it, to have the protein." Everyone swam away to look for excitement, leaving the trout alone.

The day came when a mighty earthquake made the Mississippi run backwards, and the St. Louis Arch fell over. A reporter ran down to the scene to get some eyewitness reports, but all the people there were too busy screaming. Lots of fish were at the riverbank rubbernecking, so the reporter went to interview them.

"What happened?" he asked.

"A barge full of nuclear bombs rammed into the Arch," said a muddy catfish.

"That doesn't sound very true," said the reporter, turning to the next fish.

"Megadog and Nubzilla got into a fight!" said a bulging bluegill. "They pounded each other into the ground, and that's how the Cahokia Mounds were made," he said, pointing a fin toward Illinois.

"Balderdash," said the reporter.

"Like, six hundred angry motorcycle humans came here and beat me against the Arch until my heart stopped," said the walleye. "That's also what brung down the Arch, fella! Such a loud clatter, it woke me back to life!"

"You bunch of clownfish," said the reporter. "I'm going to give you just one more chance." The honest trout was next in line.

"Apparently, a seismic event of some strength occurred, reversing the river and toppling this beloved monument," the trout said. "I saw two cars fall off the bridge, I saw a cat jump over a lady, and I saw a school bus balancing on a beer factory—see, there it is," and he pointed his fin at the bus full of terrified children teetering at the top of a building. The reporter called 9-1-1 and soon the children were rescued. The honest trout had his picture on the news, a bobblehead of him was a prize at baseball games, and the beer factory made beer with his face on it. Finally, the Arch was fixed, and at the base there was a little bronze statue of him.

When he grew old and weak, they built him a tank in the Governor's office in Jefferson City, where government workers fed him baked beans with a long baby spoon. He said a lot of honest things before he died.

7/p   Russian Daycare   c. woody

The Robot Who Attended Mardi Gras

One month each year, the button factory in Jasper, Georgia, switched over to making fake jewelry. Everyone was working overtime making plastic necklaces for Mardi Gras. The factory could make twenty necklaces per second, because, let's face it, the necklaces were junk. Just for fake jewelry season, the factory hired a robot to put necklaces in boxes. After six days of packing necklaces in boxes, the robot had some questions.

"Sir, what's Mardi Gras? Why are we doing this?"

"Hey, robot, get back to work! You just dropped a necklace. Now you have to pack twenty-one necklaces in the next second!"

"Oops," said the robot. Later another worker walked by, and the robot asked him, "Sir, where is Mardi Gras? Are you going? Why does it require so many necklaces?"

"It's a big party in New Orleans, but don't worry about it, it's not for robots," said his co-worker. The robot kept working, thinking about how, after packing all these necklaces, he really deserved to go to Mardi Gras. On his five-second break, he asked the foreman to ask the secretary to mail his paycheck to his P.O. box.

"OK, sure," said the foreman. "Now get back to work. The line started up two seconds ago—you got forty necklaces on deck and two boxes about to ship empty!"

"Oops," said the robot, who put all 40 necklaces in one box and saved the extra box. When the very last box of necklaces was packed, the robot squeezed himself into the extra box and waited.

"Hey, who left this last box laying here?" said the foreman, who lifted the last box onto the last truck. "Oof, that's a hernia in a box! What're we making, lead necklaces?"

Two days later, the robot heard yelling and felt overturned. Someone unpacked him in the middle of a crazy parade, or was it a riot? People were drinking and yelling. "Hey, cool robot!" said a fat guy who put a necklace on him. Another man barfed on the robot's feet. The robot wasn't very tall, so he couldn't see over the people. A large group of people waving underwear on sticks pushed him and he fell into a pile of garbage. A lady dropped her drink on his head. She was wearing a lot of necklaces, so he asked her if she could show him to Mardi Gras.

"THIS IS MARDI GRAS, BABY!" she screamed, and put a jester hat on him.

"Oops," said the robot. "This madness is not for robots." By the time he got to the end of the street he was wearing women's shoes and one of his arms was shorting out from some fizzy wine he'd been forced to drink. His other hand was torn off and replaced with a fork that had some kind of meat on the end. By the time he made it to the bus station one of his legs was gone. A janitor gave him a plunger to use for a leg, but he had no money to buy a bus ticket, so he had to cling to the bottom of the bus next to the hot muffler, which melted his necklace beads to his body.

When he got back to Jasper, it was almost time for work, so he reported to the button factory.

"I told you not to go to Mardi Gras," said his co-worker.

The boss got out of his fancy truck and said, "All the fake necklaces are done made, so you two are fired."

The co-worker started crying, so the robot wiped his tears with the piece of meat on his fork-hand.

"Let it all out," said the robot. "I can wipe at least twenty tears per second."

Shelli McGrath

An Unprecedented Surplus of Noselings

Nelly ran. Her feet padded softly against the ground, rhythmically pounding out a tattoo of terror. She dashed through the underbrush, scurrying left, then right, dodging under and around obstacles as they appeared before her. Behind, she could hear the human running, its two clumsy feet pounding the ground like tiny earthquakes. Her heart beat in her ears, her breath came ragged. Somewhere ahead was a hideout, a hole in the ground full of twists and turns and burrows and exits. She would lose the pursuer if she could find one of the entrances.

The body behind her stumbled, and she was able to make some headway. It was her best chance yet, and she let out the combination of squeaks that called for help. Any other animal in this wood, gen-eng or not, had to help when it heard that call, as long as they wanted to consider themselves freebeasts. Ahead, to her left, she heard a chattered response. Veering that direction, she noticed the first telltale sign of a hideaway. The scratches on the roots in the ground were meant to be invisible to the preoccupied human eye, but in her rush they had been invisible to her as well. She dove into the burrow without slowing down. Only after she had tumbled through the first passage and skittered around two bends did she slow and catch her breath. That had been too close for comfort. Her father was going to give her hell for venturing into Labcity. This time, she wouldn't be able to argue that it was perfectly safe. This time, he was right.

Another gen-eng rat approached her from ahead. He bowed his nose, but the lack of propriety in the move told her he was either a leader or impudent. She responded with the curtsy expected to a leader, feeling after her close call she should play it safe.

"Hrmph. A noseling." His voice was condescending and nasally. He turned haughtily, showing the ear growing from his hairless back. Ears had just come back into vogue, and Nelly couldn't help but smirk under her whiskers at his pomp. Obviously, this rat was taking advantage of his recent rise in popularity. It wouldn't last long, then the labs would create enough earlings to fill the need, and another organ would be declared in fashion. The hierarchy was always changing.

"Where?" he asked, without any decorum.

"Uffington-beneath-Oakgrove."

"We can get there through the underground. Follow me." The earling led her through the tunnels until she recognized her way. She squeaked her thanks to the rat and scurried off. If she hurried, she could arrive during the dinner ceremonies. Her father could not discipline her in front of the community, at least not without losing face. Allowing him time to cool down would likely play to her advantage; at least, she hoped.

As she had expected, she arrived with the clearing of places. She took a seat where he was sure to see her, and by his surly glare, she knew he had. Jacobis seemed to have aged during the day. His whiskers were white to the tip. His ragged right ear seemed withered; his left ear, rather than perking toward the conversations around him, lay limp against his head. The big toe growing out of his back needed its nail trimmed and looked pruney, as if it had been in a bath too long. He was getting old. She should have never left the burrow. He needed her here. She knew he hadn't aged that much all in the day, though he seemed ages older than this morning.

The old rat cleared his throat. He began the ceremony as always. "All freebeasts, please join me in our pledge to the commune." The crowd shuffled to their feet and recited the pledge to remain together in harmony and stand together in arms as the free animals of the land.

Their voices all joined together, lacking emphasis or enthusiasm but perfectly in tune with one another. The words were well rehearsed. Children of the commune were taught this pledge from their earliest days,

and every animal in the burrow believed these words wholeheartedly. Though the nightly recitation was much too common to sound anything but rote, each animal felt fervor for the beliefs behind it. Nelly was no exception, though tonight she was less involved than normal. She couldn't help but consider her fate. Jacobis had certainly noticed her, but he never made eye contact. She knew she was in trouble.

The dinner ceremony was fairly short; there was little more than the average community business to share. Jacobis wished everyone a good night and the commune began to thin away. Some mice stayed to gossip, smiling at their friends and relatives and chatting about inconsequential things. The room held the air of family. They were close enough that no formality was needed to end the night. After a while, Nelly and Jacobis were left alone. He sighed and sat down heavily.

"I heard you went near Labcity today."

"Yes, father." He waited, but she did not volunteer any more information.

"Nelly. News travels fast. I know you were seen by the people, that they gave chase. I heard it was quite a close call, you barely made it to Mossyrocks in time." He looked at her again, down his long nose and whiskers. Nelly didn't know what to say back. She knew she had done wrong. She knew it was her fault that she was seen and chased, and that she had endangered the Mossyrocks commune by seeking refuge in their burrows.

"I'm sorry." She squeaked meekly. This was not the response he was looking for. His eyes flashed with anger,

"You're sorry? That's all? Tell me what kind of leader you are going to be if you continue to risk your own safety for silly games! You could have been harvested! Worse than that, you led them to the Mossyrocks colony! Leaders do EVERYTHING they can to keep their people safe!" He slammed his paw down on the table, and then took a deep breath. "And, dear Nelly, that includes keeping themselves safe. You are going to lead this colony, so you need to learn how to take care of yourself before anyone will trust you to take care of them."

"Yes, father," she again replied meekly. Her whiskers drooped in shame as he shuffled to his feet. Nelly followed his lead, standing with her head bowed in disgrace.

"Well, dear. Mossyrocks is on high alert for further invasion, and they destroyed the entrance you found as well as the three nearest to it." He sighed, his whiskers dropping down. "We will sleep safe tonight, but the guard is up on full duty at Mossyrocks. What were you doing even near Labcity?"

"I was just curious, dad. I want to know why we are so different than the other freebeasts. I want to see all the places in our people's history. I didn't think anyone would notice a mere noseling."

"You are more important than you realize, my darling."

"Father, there are a million noselings. Please—."

"Yes, we have many noselings in our colony, but to the people you are a valuable asset. Nothing would make them happier than taking that nose from your back and using it in one of their espearamints. They didn't make you, but your nose is perfect. They would love to run the tests and see why. You're lucky, darling."

He sniffed some, and she realized his eyes were clouding up. "I'm so glad you're lucky. What would I do without you?" Tears began to well at his eyes, and he turned away, gruffly. He hadn't always been like this, but since the death of her mother, he had grown distant.

She couldn't stand to see him this way. She stepped forward and nuzzled his side. He tensed, then relented, turning towards her and resting his nose on the top of her head. Large wet tears rolled off the sides of his nose and splashed to the ground around her. They stayed there, motionless and speechless, until his tears dried away. She had no idea he cared this much for her. It was refreshing, in a way. They had been so distant, for so long. The moment did not last forever though, and she felt her father pulling away from her, regaining his pride and posture.

They went their separate ways to their nesting rooms in the borough. She lay down, knowing that nothing overall had changed, but at the same

72

time everything had. She was still connected to her father, they were family, and that mattered for something. She fell asleep happier than she had in months.

The happiness did not wear away. She held onto that as she went back to her daily grind. In the mornings she foraged for food to add to the stores in the borough. In the afternoons she took charge of the pups. In the evenings she helped prepare for the ceremonies. Life became pleasantly busy again. Mossyrocks had been inconvenienced, but word came that no lasting harm had been done. They made new entrances to replace the ones they had destroyed. Her father regained his aloof manner to her, but she had been reassured of his care, and it held through all his cold greetings.

One afternoon, on her way from the nursery to the storage dens, things changed again. Two adolescent earlings, a young noseling, and several juvenile mash-ups were crowding around another young mouse with a prominent bulbous nose poking out of his back. He was dramatically telling a tall tale about an adventure he had had outside the borough. He was rigorously detailing the terrors of nearing the Labcity as she approached. Though he was keeping his voice low enough that it would not echo through the tunnels, he was so engaged in the story that he did not seem to notice her approach.

"And then the clumsy human sign-test reached out to catch me, and I bit him on the finger!"

The crowd of young mice gasped dramatically.

"I scurried up him and rested on his nose just long enough for him to react. He slapped as I jumped, and managed to hit himself so hard in the nose that his lifeblood rushed out of it in a great torrent!"

One of the youngest mash-ups squeaked in terror.

"I gallantly leaped off of his shoulder, having thoroughly slayed him, and left Labcity triumphant in his demise!"

The young mice burst into squeaks and stamps of appreciation. Just then, the earling stepped back into Nelly.

73

"Oh, 'scuse me miss nelly" he said, overly loud. "we were just get-ting on our way!" His voice carried, and the other mice scurried away. Nelly turned, and he took advantage of the moment and ran off himself. Nelly shook her head to herself, and ambled off toward the storage bins. She didn't give the scene any more thought, but was surprised less than an hour later, when one of the noselings from the crowd showed up.

He claimed he was picking up supplies for the nursery, and Nel-ly immediately knew something was up. She had just sent them their regular order. Playing the role of an interested bystander, Nelly drew out from the noseling that he was off on an adventure. He seemed to think it would carry an air of extreme danger. Nelly did not mind playing along, remembering her own childhood jaunts through dark tunnels in search of feats of peril. It was only when he accidentally mentioned a sign-test that she grew worried. When he scurried off, Nelly mumbled an apology to the mouse overseeing stocks, and followed him discretely.

The noseling picked up a satchel just around the first bend, then scur-ried off, heading directly to the main exit. Nelly chattered behind him, but he was too caught up in his adventure. She would have to catch him to turn him back. Nelly hurried after, feeling slightly winded—he was younger and much more agile. While Nelly had to slow down for obsta-cles and pick her way through, the noseling barely curbed his step and dove through the underbrush with abandon. Before she realized it, they were crossing the out-most borders of the commune.

Nelly chattered at him again, but the noseling still managed to not notice her in the slightest. She slowed her step, remembering the words of her father. She could not, she should not pass that boundary—yet she knew the noseling would be in danger. Inspiration hit her like a flash: "Leaders do everything they can to keep their people safe!" He had said it! She must go! With new energy, Nelly rushed out of the cover of under-brush and after the young mouse.

The noseling ahead finally slowed at the first fence. He cowered down under a dandelion leaf and looked at the fence ahead. Nelly was able to use this momentary pause and rushed to him. The noseling jumped a full three inches off the ground when he heard her.

"Watcha doin' here, Miss Nelly?"

"I followed you, dearling. What is your proper name?"

"Aaron."

"And what are you doing, so far from safety, Aaron?"

"I came for the adventure! Jamesey told me all about what Labcity is like and I want to make my mark! I've come to free some of the imprisoned pups just like he did."

"Dearling, did you see any of the pups he claimed to free?"

"Well … no, but that's cause they was in the infirmatory!"

"Aaron … dearling … I spend my afternoons in the infirmatory some days. I have heard of no new pups. I think Jamesey was … well … sometimes stories sound nicer than reality, dearling."

"No! Jamesey wouldn't a lied!"

"I'm not saying he lied, so much, as, well, dearling …." At that moment a tremor in the ground sent them both flat on their bellies. A human had crept up to the other side of the fence, and had dropped to its knees to look at them beneath the dandelion leaves.

"It's just a human pup, don't be afraid, and don't move a muscle." Nelly whispered, fiercely. Aaron trembled. She saw his eyes had gone glossy. Things were worse than she had thought. What could she do, though? There was no way to break a mouse from a panic, and he was too large to restrain if … no—*when* he bolted.

"Aaron … Aaron, my dearling … Aaron, please …." Her whispers had no effect on the mouse. His shaking increased, and his ears slowly drooped back on his head.

"Aaron!" she whispered louder, but instead of breaking him from his trance he jerked forward. With a great leap he took off, at a full tilt. He bounded three giant leaps forward before running head first into a pole holding the fence up. He fell to the ground, knocked out cold.

"Mousey! With a nose!" The human pup pressed his face against the

fence, and reached through the metal diamonds with his fingers to softly touch Aaron's head.

Nelly burst forward. She nipped the human pup on the tip of his finger, and he immediately let out a wail louder than any wolf howl she had ever heard in her lifetime. She picked Aaron up by the scruff of his neck and began dragging him away. It was slow work; he was at least a third her size. She gave a huge heave and pulled him back under the dandelion. She felt the rumbling of the earth before she saw the full-grown humans running toward the human pup, who was still wailing relentlessly, louder than any sound she had ever heard; the pitch of its cry made her lay her ears flat against her back, and she could feel the nostrils of the nose on her back flaring in defense at the sound.

Desperately, she tugged at Aaron again, pulling him back several more steps. She was still unimaginably far from the forest. Blood trickled from Aaron's mouth. She tugged and jerked at his limp body, pulling him farther and faster than she thought possible with her own small form. The full-grown humans had reached their young, and were kneeling around him, crooning in their strange language at the child. One picked him up and brought him back toward their above-ground tunnel. The other picked up a large stick and began poking through the fence at the ground. Nelly tugged harder, it was sure to see her soon, and she couldn't make a break for it without leaving Aaron.

The human spotted her, and made a loud call that sounded close to the wail that appeared from the human pup, only lower in decibel. Nelly jerked Aaron back another few inches. The human held the stick up above his head, then flung it at her with more power than she thought possible. The stick hit the ground directly in front of her, and its other end smashed down against the nose on her back. She felt a dampness on her side, and by stretching her neck could see that red was flowing from her nose's nostrils. The nose itself was at an odd angle on her back, and turning a strange shade of purplish blue that she had only seen on flowers before now.

The human, seeming happy with this, turned away and stomped back toward its tunnel. Nelly, despite the exhaustion and pain, continued to tug Aaron, inch by inch, across the forest floor. Eventually she reached the outer patrolled border of their commune. With a few squeaks, she drew the guard, and they carried her weary body as well as Aaron back to the infirmatory. She passed out on the way.

She was still unconscious when the nurse-mouse pronounced Aaron dead; having cracked his skull, he did not survive his impact with the fence pole. She was not yet awake when one of the largest intern mice was brought in to re-break and straighten her mangled nose, which would forever carry a bump that displayed her braveness to the colony, though only reminded her of her failure. She wasn't conscious when three of Aaron's closest pup friends came forward, having known of his plan, validating her story before she told it to anyone. She eventually did awake. Her father was there, had been there, and would be by her side throughout her recovery. Somehow, that made all the difference.

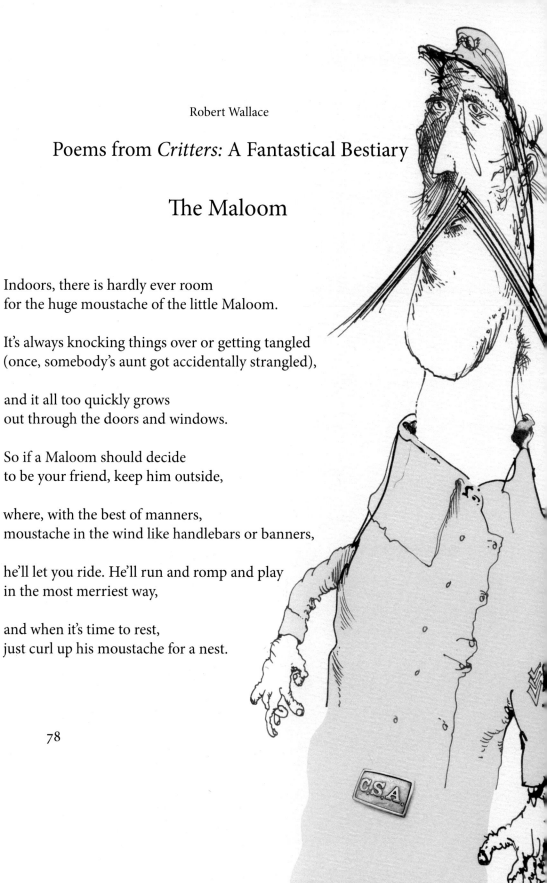

Robert Wallace

Poems from *Critters:* A Fantastical Bestiary

The Maloom

Indoors, there is hardly ever room
for the huge moustache of the little Maloom.

It's always knocking things over or getting tangled
(once, somebody's aunt got accidentally strangled),

and it all too quickly grows
out through the doors and windows.

So if a Maloom should decide
to be your friend, keep him outside,

where, with the best of manners,
moustache in the wind like handlebars or banners,

he'll let you ride. He'll run and romp and play
in the most merriest way,

and when it's time to rest,
just curl up his moustache for a nest.

The Bagnol

The Bagnol never hears
because he has no ears.

Without a nose,
he never smells where it is he goes.

And lacking taste,
the finest dinner would be a waste.

That he doesn't see is no surprise
since he also has no eyes.

Nor does he have the sense of touch.
Nothing gets to the Bagnol much.

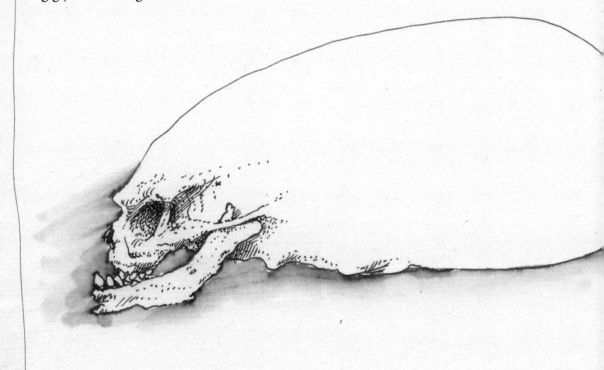

The Foom

The dangerous Foom,
about the size of a dentist's waiting room

(a baby's the size of a closet),
is mostly jaws. It

swims about wherever it takes a notion,
in pond or ocean,

and may even surface like a sub
in somebody's bathtub.

Don't worry, though: it never
ever

—when it surfaces, snaps, and dives—
eats anything but dentists and their wives,

especially on vacation, in pretty
boats bobbing off Atlantic City

or on Lake Winnipesaukee, sailing.
One chomp, and they're bailing.

The next chomp—don't look, though.
The point is, it's important to know,

as is the case of the dangerous Foom,
dangerous to whom?

The Xalif

The eyes of the Xalif are located on his toes
(front and back, he has twenty of those),

so he can see exactly where each foot goes.
But—he keeps stubbing his nose.

The Dwilg

Disliking company, even his own,
the blue-tusked Dwilg lives all alone

in a burrow far, far, far from town
and way, way, down,

and he'd move in a minute
if he could find a place without himself in it.

The Quib

A half-inch butterfly, bright
as brittlest glass, eight blues and a white,

with green-jewel eyes and green antennae,
wee-er than any,

the Quib balances upon leaves or things
and sings and sings,

although
at first you would not think so.

For the note of the Quib is pure and tiny,
so sunshinily fine he

can only be heard by ears as minimal
as his song is thin and small.

If you listen, however, it's there—
a tinkle sweetening the summer air.

The Plockle

A marvelous disappearer,
fast as breath on a mirror—

there's no way you can keep a Plockle.
Not even a cage or chains a lock'll.

Though solid as ice,
with gray and frosty eyelashes, gray and frosty eyes,

he's able just to melt and trickle out
under doors, or through bars however stout.

If you put him in a tank or pool,
shortly you'll

find that, like water, he also turns to vapor,
this wonderful escaper,

and riding off mysteriously in air,
condenses himself elsewhere.

84

The Rotosaur

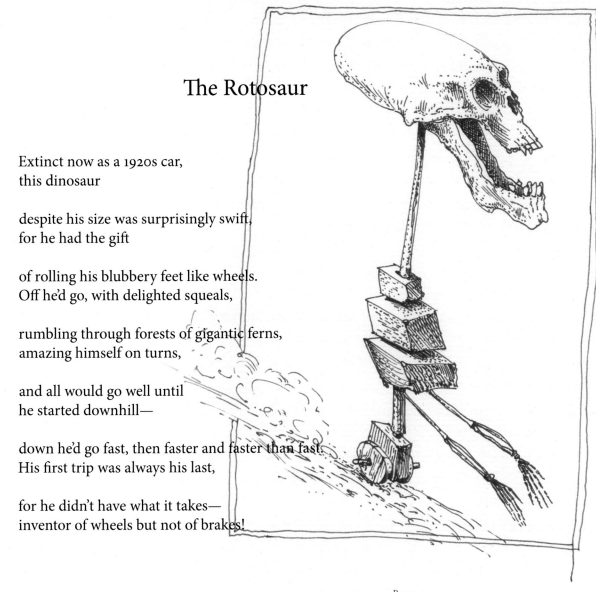

Extinct now as a 1920s car,
this dinosaur

despite his size was surprisingly swift,
for he had the gift

of rolling his blubbery feet like wheels.
Off he'd go, with delighted squeals,

rumbling through forests of gigantic ferns,
amazing himself on turns,

and all would go well until
he started downhill—

down he'd go fast, then faster and faster than fast.
His first trip was always his last,

for he didn't have what it takes—
inventor of wheels but not of brakes!

Вротозавр

Mark I. West

The Intersection of Fantasy and Social Commentary in Roald Dahl's *Fantastic Mr. Fox*

Roald Dahl is remembered as one of the Twentieth Century's most successful writers of fantasy stories for children, but his reputation as a fantasist belies his keen interest in writing about the real world. In many of his fantasy books, he comments in a satirical way on real-world trends and topics. One of his favorite targets is the popularity of television, which he mocks in *Charlie and the Chocolate Factory* (1964) and *Matilda* (1988). He also takes pleasure in poking fun at military officers. Toward the end of *The BFG* (1982), for example, Dahl portrays the heads of the British Army and the Air Force as a couple of boastful buffoons who are more concerned about winning medals than solving problems. In fact, there are touches of social commentary in almost all of Dahl's children's books, but this trait is especially pronounced in *Fantastic Mr. Fox* (1970).

Fantastic Mr. Fox can be read as a multileveled story. On one level, *Fantastic Mr. Fox* is an animal fantasy story with trickster elements. On another level, however, *Fantastic Mr. Fox* is a highly satirical tale that not only criticizes contemporary values and social conventions, but also questions the ethical underpinnings of modern capitalistic society. At its core, this book undermines societal values concerning private property, and as such it can be interpreted as one of the most radical of Dahl's children's books.

Shortly after the publication of *Fantastic Mr. Fox* in 1970, Margery Fisher gave the book a positive review in which she called it a "robust tale" and described Mr. Fox as a "worthy descendant of the medieval

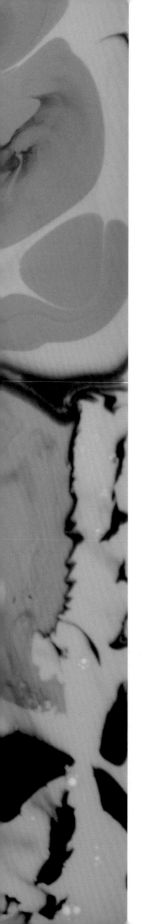

Renard" (1716). By drawing a connection between Mr. Fox and the character of Renard (sometimes spelled Reynard), Fisher's review places *Fantastic Mr. Fox* within a useful cultural context. Like *Fantastic Mr. Fox*, the medieval tales about Renard feature an anthropomorphic fox that functions as a trickster character. However, the connections between Dahl's story and these medieval tales go much deeper than these surface similarities. One of the foremost authorities on the medieval Renard tales is Patricia Terry. Known for translating these tales from Old French into English, Terry stresses that the original authors often infused their tales with an anti-establishment theme:

> The authors were anything but pedantic; nor were they out to write the simple tales for children extracted from their work by later bowdlerizers. They attacked, with gusto and a subterranean idealism, the government of their country, its legal system, its Church, the formalities of feudalism, the hollow protection offered the underprivileged, and the unredeemed brutality of peasants. They put us on the side of a revolutionary individual who is, however, no social reformer but a murderer and a thief. (3)

Terry goes on to argue that, though these tales have political undertones, they cannot be accurately described as political fables. In many ways, Renard is much like a real fox, and his conflicts with the society around him are similar to the real conflicts between foxes and humans. Renard's tendency to raid henhouses is certainly grounded in real life. As Terry points out, "When the characters are clothed in real fur and real feathers, not only is their experience of life, insofar as it resembles our own, an entertainment, but there is further charm in those moments when we are reminded, by a gesture of wing or tail, that they are animals" (3).

   Like Renard, Dahl's Mr. Fox is often in conflict with human society, and this conflict often has something to do with poultry. The central plotline of Dahl's story revolves around an ongoing tension between

88

Mr. Fox and three nasty farmers named Boggis, Bunce, and Bean, all of whom raise poultry. These farmers are not only mean, but they are also physically repulsive. Bean, for example, is so filthy that "his ear holes [are] clogged with all kinds of muck and wax and bits of chewing gum and dead flies" (15). Boggis, Bunce, and Bean do battle with Mr. Fox and his family throughout the story. The farmers want to kill Mr. Fox because he regularly steals their poultry to feed his family. The farmers find the entrance to the hole where the foxes live and attempt to shoot Mr. Fox when he leaves the hole. When this plan fails, they decide to dig the foxes out. The foxes, however, simply dig in deeper. Finally, the farmers lay siege to the foxhole with the intention of starving the foxes to death. Mr. Fox eventually solves this problem by digging tunnels underneath the buildings in which the poultry are kept, thus making it possible for him to feed his family without going near the entrance to the foxhole.

The conflict between the foxes and the farmers is made more dramatic by the characters' strong emotional reactions to the events in the story. Each time the foxes get away, the farmers react by becoming "more furious and more obstinate and more determined than ever not to give up" (21). Although the farmers seem fairly comical in the beginning of the story, their increasing fanaticism transforms them into formidable villains. In contrast, there is a sense of pathos in the foxes' reactions to the campaign to eradicate them. Their physical and emotional sufferings are convincingly described, and this helps the reader care about their plight. Also, the reader cannot help but admire the foxes' bravery and unflagging devotion to each other.

Although the plot focuses on the conflict between Mr. Fox and the three poultry farmers, the book also deals with two other overarching conflicts. *Fantastic Mr. Fox* can be seen as a tale about the conflict between the natural environment and the more artificial environment created by modern humans. The book also relates to the conflict between those who possess extensive private property and those who do not. In this sense, the book touches on the topic of class conflict.

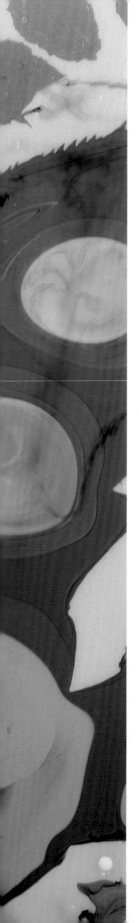

Dahl's interest in the conflict between nature and humans predates the publication of *Fantastic Mr. Fox*. He published a children's book titled *The Magic Finger* in 1966, in which he takes up the topic of hunting as a recreational sport. In this story, human hunters find themselves in the position of being hunted, and as a result they develop a sense of empathy for the former targets of their blood sport. *The Magic Finger* uses fantasy elements to explore the relationship between humans and wild animals, and it implies that humans should make more of an effort to co-exist with wild animals. This theme also figures in *Fantastic Mr. Fox*, which is the very next book that Dahl wrote after *The Magic Finger*.

Mr. Fox and most of the other animal characters in *Fantastic Mr. Fox* are anthropomorphized, but they are still portrayed as real wild animals. In many ways, Dahl's depiction of these animal characters is similar to Beatrix Potter's depiction of animals in her Peter Rabbit books. Potter's animals can talk, and they sometimes wear clothing, but they still live the lives of actual animals—so, too, with Dahl's animal characters. Mr. Fox retains many of the traits of real foxes. He lives in an underground den, just as many real foxes do. He is an adept digger, just as real foxes are. As is often the case with real foxes, he maintains a relationship with his immediate family. And, like many real foxes, he lives in close proximity to humans and often takes advantage of food sources associated with humans. Thus, the conflict between the poultry farmers and Mr. Fox can also be seen as being emblematic of the conflict between humans and wild animals.

The human characters in *Fantastic Mr. Fox* operate their farms in such a way that they are not in harmony with nature and the wild animals that live in the woods nearby. These wealthy farmers run large, highly specialized businesses in which the raising of poultry is transformed into a mass-production operation. These men see the wild animals that live near their farms as nuisances that must be eliminated. For their part, Mr. Fox and the other animal characters recognize the farmers as threats to their very existence. At one point Mr. Fox says to Mr. Badger, "Look, Boggis and Bunce and Bean are out to kill us, you realize that, I hope? … But we're not going to stoop to their level. We don't want to kill them" (46). As Dahl makes clear in the context of his story, the conflict between the humans and the animals is caused by the farmers' disregard for the natural environment and the wild animals that are part of that environment.

The conflict between the farmers and the animal characters also involves the issue of private property. The farmers not only own large tracts of land, but they also view everything that is on their land as their private property. Thus, when Mr. Fox helps himself to a few of the thousands of chickens kept by Boggis, the farmers see this act as stealing private property. Mr. Fox, however, has a different view. Toward the end of the story, when Mr. Badger questions Mr. Fox about helping himself to poultry, Mr. Fox replies, "My dear old furry frump, do you know anyone in the whole world who wouldn't swipe a few chickens if their children were starving?' (45). Mr. Fox clearly places greater value on providing for his family than on respecting private property.

Mr. Fox's attitude toward stealing concerned Dahl's editor, Bob Bernstein. In Storyteller: The Authorized Biography of Roald Dahl, Donald Sturrock examines the correspondence between Bernstein and Dahl, and Sturrock reports that Bernstein asked Dahl to revise the story in such a way that it would not seem to condone stealing. Dahl, however, "did not budge on the issue of theft." According to Sturrock, Dahl sent Bernstein a letter in which he wrote, "Foxes live by stealing" (qtd. in Sturrock 446). Of course, Dahl prevailed in this dispute. Bernstein worried that this aspect of the book would undercut the sales of the book, but this concern proved to be unfounded since the book "quickly became a bestseller" (Sturrock 446).

While Dahl referred to the behavior of real foxes when justifying his refusal to edit out the sections of Fantastic Mr. Fox that deal with Mr. Fox's poultry raids, there was another reason for Dahl's refusal. Dahl had, to quote Sturrock, a "poacher's mentality" (444). In some ways, Mr. Fox can be seen as a poacher, and, for Dahl, this trait is not necessarily a bad thing.

Dahl practically celebrates poaching in *Danny, The Champion of the World*, which came out just a few years after the publication of *Fantastic Mr. Fox*. In *Danny, The Champion of the World*, Danny, a nine-year-old boy, and his father engage in the "exciting sport" of poaching pheasants from a vast stretch of property owned by the owner of a huge brewery (Danny 29).

Both *Fantastic Mr. Fox* and *Danny, The Champion of the World* present poaching in a positive light, and in so doing these stories suggest that not all of society's rules are equally just. These books imply that it is not ethically wrong to disobey laws that are designed solely to protect the interests of the privileged class. These stories make it clear that there are risks involved in disobeying these rules but that running a risk is not the same thing as being unethical. The readers of these stories come away with the impression that it is more important to provide for one's family and to practice kindness than to follow societal rules and conventions.

Although *Fantastic Mr. Fox* challenges some of the core values of modern capitalistic society, it would be a stretch to view Mr. Fox as a social reformer or as a political revolutionary. Like Renard, Mr. Fox is not out to change the world. He is interested primarily in himself and his immediate family. His story, like the tales of Renard, abounds with examples of bravery and cleverness, but he is also a character who enjoys his creature comforts and who does not worry too much about legalistic matters. Mr. Fox takes an almost hedonistic pleasure in eating good food, and he enjoys the game-like aspects of outwitting his adversaries. In these ways, he is very much like his predecessor Renard.

However, even though *Fantastic Mr. Fox* is not a story about political or social change, it nonetheless includes a critique of modern capitalistic society. This story calls into question the values associated with what has come to be known as agribusiness. The large, specialized farms that figure in this story clearly present a danger to the environment, including the local wildlife. Dahl implies that the owners of these farms are so motivated by greed that they are oblivious to how their actions are harmful to nature. The book does not endorse the abolition of private property, but it does undercut the importance of property rights. Mr. Fox clearly places greater value on protecting his family than on respecting private property. At its core, the story suggests that there is more to morality than obeying societal rules.

Works Cited

Dahl, Roald. *Fantastic Mr. Fox*. New York: Knopf, 1970. Print.
———. *Danny, The Champion of the World*. New York: Knopf, 1982. Print.
Fisher, Margery. Rev. of *Fantastic Mr. Fox. Growing Point*. April 1971: 1716. Print.
Sturrock, Donald. *Storyteller: The Authorized Biography of Roald Dahl*. New York: Simon & Schuster, 2010. Print.
Terry, Patricia. *Renard the Fox*. Boston: Northeastern UP, 1983. Print.

Teddybear by Jewel Wakeman

She prepares the Child for the World
Help her to help prepare the World for the Child

What does War mean to These?

Joel D. Chaston

"Every College Needs a Chair of Kewpieology": Rose O'Neill's Carnivalesque Kewpies

Mrs. Hauser came towards them puffing like a locomotive.…
Under her arm she carried two huge pink Kewpie dolls; one with
a red ballet skirt and one with green.

"I won 'em," said Mrs. Hauser, grunting as she let herself
carefully and gradually sink to the ground. "One at the coconut
shy and one at the weight-lifting thing. You'd think they'd have
better prizes than Kewpie dolls! Garnet, you can have the green
one, and Citronella can keep the red." (Elizabeth Enright, *Thimble
Summer* 122)

In Elizabeth Enright's Newbery Award-winning children's novel, *Thimble
Summer* (1937), a minor character, Mrs. Hauser, wins several "carnival"
games at a county fair in Southwestern Wisconsin. Like thousands of
Depression-era fairgoers, Mrs. Hauser receives Kewpie dolls for winning two of the games, prizes she clearly disdains. By the late 1930's (the
setting for *Thimble Summer*), the popularity of Rose O'Neill's Kewpies,
which debuted in 1909, had begun to wane. Cheap celluloid versions had
replaced the original porcelain dolls based on the characters of O'Neill's
poems and drawings and, like Mrs. Hauser, a few cultural critics had
begun to attack the Kewpies as cloyingly cute and over-commercialized.

As Shelly Armitage tells the story, the Kewpies had their inception in
the cupid-like decorations which O'Neill, then an aspiring commercial
artist, used in her early magazine illustrations. Eventually, Edward Bok,
editor of *Ladies Home Journal,* invited O'Neill to "develop these cupids

95

into full-page multiple-image features and promised to find someone to write the accompanying text. O'Neill agreed but then decided she would compose the narrative, in verse form, herself. She created Kewpieville, an enchanted realm of joy and selflessness, filling it with Kewpie characters" (42). In December 1909, Bok published O'Neill's illustrated poem, "The Kewpies' Christmas Frolic." The Kewpies were an instant success and were regularly featured in *Ladies Home Journal,* as well as other popular magazines, including *Good Housekeeping, Women's Home Journal, Companion,* and *Delineator.* The growing demand for Kewpies led to books about the Kewpies, such as *The Kewpies and Dottie Darling* (1910), *The Kewpies, Their Book* (1912), and *Scootles in Kewpieville* (1936). Three years after the publication of the first Kewpie poem, the first Kewpie dolls were manufactured. O'Neill sculpted the models for these dolls and personally oversaw their production by J. D. Kestner, a German company. Originally made of bisque porcelain, the Kewpie doll later appeared in celluloid, plastic, and cardboard cutout versions.

O'Neill's creation would regain some of its popularity in the last half of the Twentieth Century. Modern versions of the Kewpie doll are now popular with contemporary doll collectors, prompting the creation of the International Rose O'Neill Foundation in 1967. The Rose O'Neill Museum (Springfield, Missouri) and Bonniebrook Gallery, Museum, and Homestead (Walnut Shade, Missouri) draw visitors from around the world, largely due to an ongoing interest in the Kewpie.

O'Neill's cherubs also live on as symbols and mascots for various organizations and brands of merchandise. For example, the Kewpie serves as the mascot for David H. Hickman High School in Columbia, Missouri, and appears in advertisements for a popular brand of mayonnaise in Japan. Unfortunately, contemporary attitudes towards Kewpies are generally based on knockoffs of O'Neill's Kewpie dolls that, despite their variety of outfits, often have the same facial expression. As a result, much of the playful spirit and subversive nature of O'Neill's original Kewpies is no longer readily apparent.

The Kewpies and the College

Verses and Pictures
by Rose O'Neill

Every College should have
a Chair of Kewpiology

The Bookman has a strong proclivity
Toward undue cerebral activity.
And since 'twas plain his bookish tendency
Was slowly gaining the ascendency,
Wag stirred the Kewps to capers antical,
Which made the studious Bookman frantical

Said he: "I have no time for squandering;
You Kewpish coots disturb my pondering;
All by myself I'll go off wandering!
I'll seek the heady hospitality
Of some renowned 'highbrow' sodality
That welcomes intellectuality!"

At this the Kewps flocked round him coaxingly.
But, dears, he went—albeit hoaxingly.
He left in love and not in anger, pets,
Explaining first with patient languor, pets,
That their extreme and marked frivolity
Was ruining his mental quality.

"But, Bookman," barked the Kewpish terrier,
"Please don't grow any literarier,
'Cause Kewps exist to make life merrier!"

The Information Kewpie,
had a hard time studying.

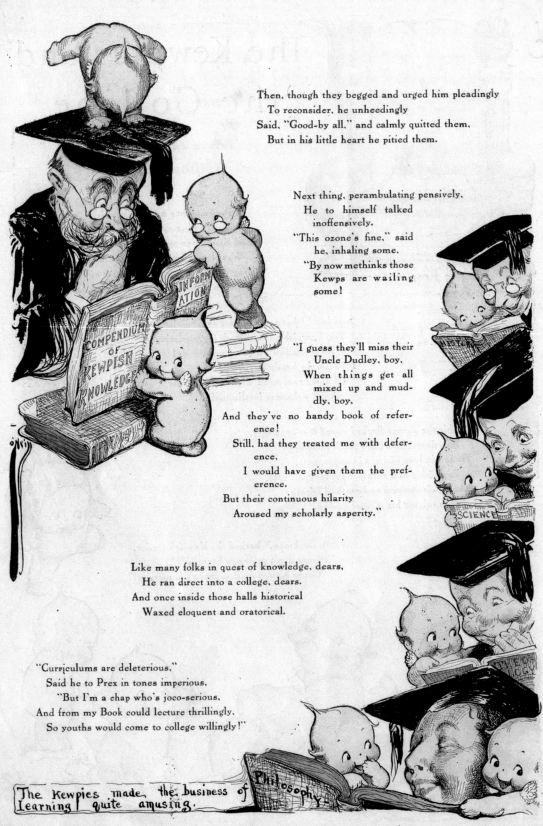

3

Then, though they begged and urged him pleadingly
  To reconsider, he unheedingly
Said, "Good-by all," and calmly quitted them,
  But in his little heart he pitied them.

Next thing, perambulating pensively,
  He to himself talked
    inoffensively.
"This ozone's fine," said
  he, inhaling some,
  "By now methinks those
    Kewps are wailing
      some!

"I guess they'll miss their
  Uncle Dudley, boy,
    When things get all
      mixed up and mud-
      dly, boy,
And they've no handy book of refer-
  ence!
  Still, had they treated me with defer-
  ence,
    I would have given them the pref-
      erence.
But their continuous hilarity
  Aroused my scholarly asperity."

Like many folks in quest of knowledge, dears,
  He ran direct into a college, dears.
And once inside those halls historical
  Waxed eloquent and oratorical.

"Curriculums are deleterious,"
  Said he to Prex in tones imperious,
    "But I'm a chap who's joco-serious,
And from my Book could lecture thrillingly,
  So youths would come to college willingly!"

The Kewpies made the business of
learning quite amusing.

In "Portraits of Womanhood in the Artwork of Rose O'Neill" (2009), an article in an earlier volume of *Moon City Review,* James S. Baumlin and Lanette Cadle explore O'Neill's career as a writer, artist, and activist, a career that encompassed much more than her Kewpies. Much of O'Neill's art and writing for adults reflects her interest in politics (including women's suffrage) and social issues, especially those concerning women and children (Fig. 1). However, many of O'Neill's early Kewpie poems and drawings reflect the interests and concerns of her later, "adult" work. At the same time, they share many of the subversive qualities of earlier children's texts.

According to Alison Lurie's *Don't Tell the Grown-ups: Subversive Children's Literature* (1990), "Most of the great works of juvenile literature are subversive in one way or another: they express ideas and emotions not generally approved of or even recognized at the time; they make fun of honored figures and piously held beliefs; and they view social pretenses with clear-eyed directness, remarking—as in Andersen's famous tale—that the emperor has no clothes" (4). Several recent critics have noted the subversive nature of the Kewpies, which also reflects Mikhail Bakhtin's concept of the carnivalesque (the subject of an essay by Angelia Northrip-Rivera in this volume).

In her introduction to O'Neill's autobiography, Miriam Formanek-Brunell addresses the carnivalesque ancestry of the Kewpies, who are "an amalgamation of dominant forms, genres, and themes drawn from popular and high culture." She suggests that "the Kewpie is informed by ancient Greek mythology (Cupid), Christian iconography (angels), and Irish folk culture (elves and pixies)," but that "its origins are also quintessentially American. Although raised on ancient and medieval history, art, literature, and European folktales, O'Neill nevertheless saw magical beings—along with complementary monstrous forms—in the enchanted Missouri Ozarks that shaped her best-known work" (7). Kewpies, Formanek-Brunell explains, are "free-thinking intellectuals who analyze and evaluate the impact of

American culture on the rich and poor, native born and immigrant, adult and child" (18).

Sianne Ngai supports Formanek-Brunell's interpretation of the Kewpies in "The Cuteness of the Avant-Garde," an essay on the scholarly backlash against art and material culture that appears "cute, glamorous, whimsical, luscious, cozy." As one of her examples, Ngai notes the "physical vigor" of O'Neill's Kewpies, who "were depicted as energetic social reformers who rescued children and even educated mothers about the welfare of children … " (819).

This reprinting of two of O'Neill's Kewpie illustrated poems, "The Kewpies and the College" (1916) and "The School of Jollity" (1918)—both for *Good Housekeeping* (Figs. 2-6)—provides contemporary readers with a glimpse at the subversive side of O'Neill's cherubs. These poems gently satirize academia, education, and literary criticism, as well as the attitudes of some adults towards children. (Apparently, O'Neill's Kewpies may be relevant to some contemporary readers.) Also reproduced are two original pen-and-ink drawings (Figs. 7-10) that O'Neill had prepared for magazine publication. These unique pieces give insight into her artistic process. The images are drawn first, placed along the page's borders; once the visual composition is settled, the poetry comes next—often in O'Neill's distinctively art-deco calligraphic hand. Note that the drawings selected feature themes of childhood literacy: whereas the human children are shown reading with various expressions of sorrow, puzzlement, and resistance, the Kewpies embrace literacy as joyfully-liberating play.

We are grateful to David O'Neill, great-nephew of Rose O'Neill and director of the Rose O'Neill Museum in Springfield, who provided the images of O'Neill's published poems and original, unpublished art. Enjoy.

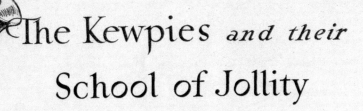

The Kewpies *and their*
School of Jollity

By Rose O'Neill

KEWPIE SCHOOL OF JOLLITY

BLAK-BORED

Mr. GRUMP

HA + HA = HA HA!

Mr. GRIN

INFORMATION on LAUGHTER, GRINS, CHUCKLES, GIGGLES.

Once upon a time the Kewpies decided to set up a school for the study of Jollity. They taught gayety in all its branches, and had especially trained Professors of Laughter, and

JOKES

march 1918

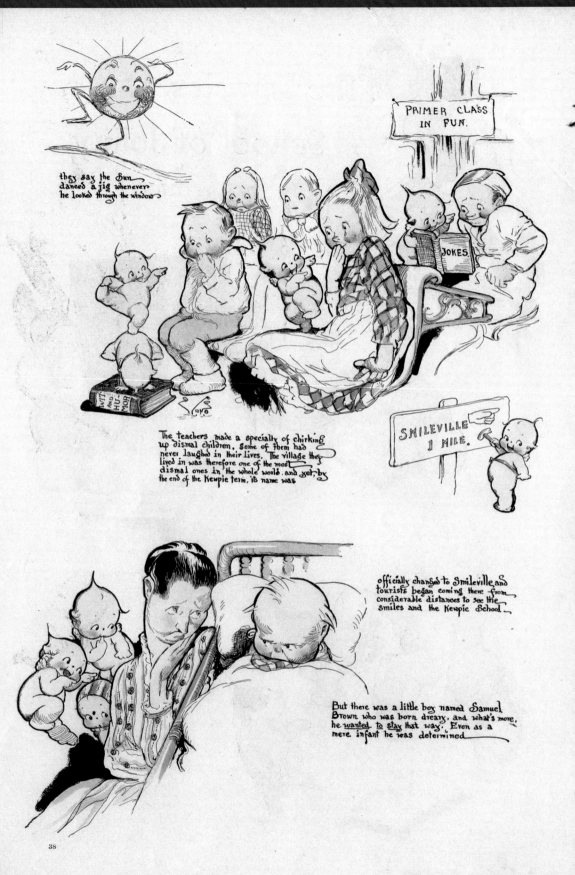

they say the Sun danced a jig whenever he looked through the window

JOKES

WIT AND HUMOR

The teachers made a specialty of chirking up dismal children. Some of them had never laughed in their lives. The village they lived in was therefore one of the most dismal ones in the whole world, and yet, by the end of the Kewpie term, its name was

SMILEVILLE 1 MILE.

officially changed to Smileville and tourists began coming there from considerable distances to see the smiles and the Kewpie School.

But there was a little boy named Samuel Brown who was born dreary, and what's more, he wanted to stay that way. Even as a mere infant he was determined

Works Cited

Armitage, Shelly. *Kewpies and Beyond: The World of Rose O'Neill.* Jackson, MS: UP of Mississippi, 1994. Print.

Baumlin, James S., and Lanette Cadle. "Portraits of Womanhood in the Artwork of Rose O'Neill." *Moon City Review 2009.* Springfield, MO: Moon City, 2009. 190-225. Print.

Enright, Elizabeth. *Thimble Summer.* 1938. New York: Dell, 1966. Print.

Formanek-Brunell, Miriam. Introduction. *The Story of Rose O'Neill: An Autobiography.* Columbia, MO: U of Missouri P, 1997. 1-20. Print.

Lurie, Allison. *Don't Tell the Grown-Ups: Subversive Children's Literature.* New York: Little Brown, 1990. Print.

Ngai, Sianne. "The Cuteness of the Avant-Garde." *Critical Inquiry* 31 (2005): 811-847. Print.

Sweeney, Meghan M. "'Like a Vanishing World': The Role of the County Fair in Three Depression-Era Children's Books." *Children's Literature Association Quarterly* 32.2 (2007): 142-162. Print.

Fig 1. "What does War Mean to These?" Pen-and-ink drawing for an anti-war poster (ca. 1917). O'Neill's pacifism is given full rein in this sketch, which contrasts the heroic woman's fierce protectiveness with the innocence of the suckling child.

Figs. 2-3. "The Kewpies and the College." Pages from the October 1916 issue of *Good Housekeeping.*

Figs. 4-6. "The School of Jollity." Pages from the March 1918 issue of *Good Housekeeping.*

Fig. 7. "Kewpies in the Lap of Learning." Pen-and-ink drawing (ca. 1916). In this original sketch, O'Neill combines the strength and sensuousness of a goddess-mother with the innocence of her darling Kewpies.

Fig. 8. "Our Folks Insist that we Must Study Things." Pen-and-ink drawing (ca. 1918) accepted "for future use" by *Good Housekeeping*. Hovering above, the Kewpies watch children struggling to read. Why the human children's sense of boredom, puzzlement, even punishment? It's because they haven't been taught "the Kewpie way"—which is to treat learning as a form of play that awakens childish wonder over the world and its mysteries/delights. As O'Neill's narrator says in "The Kewpies and the College," "Kewpies made the business of learning quite amusing."

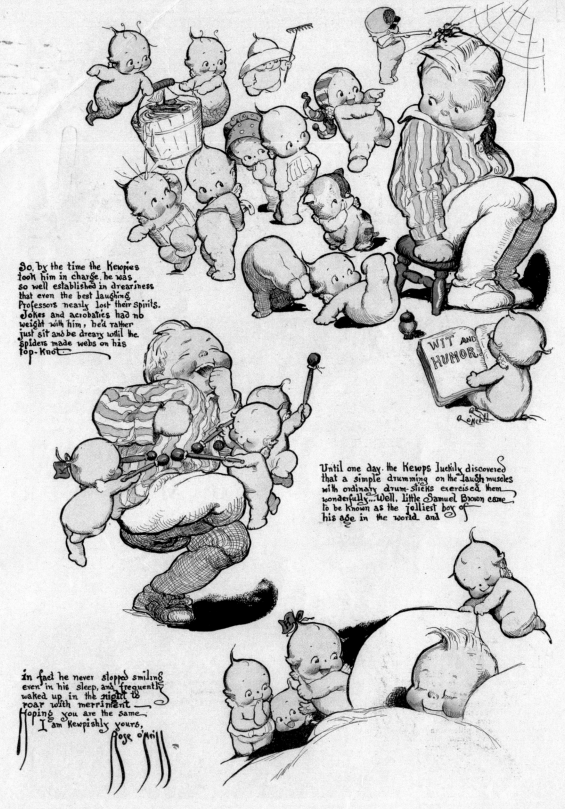

So, by the time the Kewpies
took him in charge, he was
so well established in dreariness
that even the best laughing
Professors nearly lost their spirits.
Jokes and acrobatics had no
weight with him, he'd rather
just sit and be dreary while the
spiders made webs on his
top-knot.

WIT AND
HUMOR

Until one day, the Kewps luckily discovered
that a simple drumming on the laugh muscles
with ordinary drum-sticks exercised them
wonderfully...Well, little Samuel Brown came
to be known as the jolliest boy of
his age in the world and

In fact he never stopped smiling
even in his sleep, and frequently
waked up in the night to
roar with merriment.
Hoping you are the same,
I am Kewpishly yours,
Rose O'Neill

Kewpies in the lap of Learning.

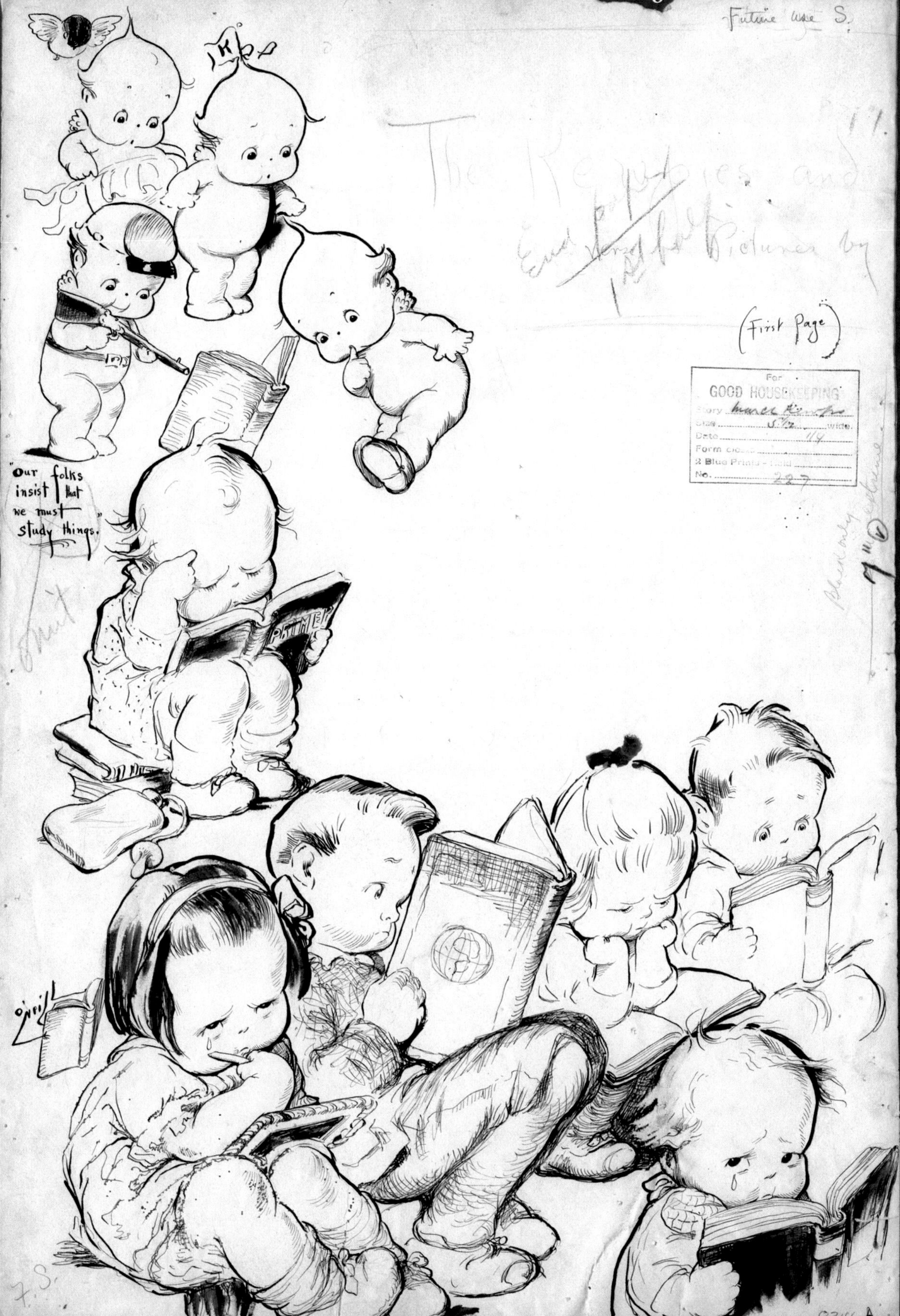

8

Future use S.

The Kewpies and

(First Page)

For
GOOD HOUSEKEEPING

"Our folks
insist that
we must
study things."

O'Neill

8341 A

Illustration by James S. Baumlin

III. Rewritings and Revisions

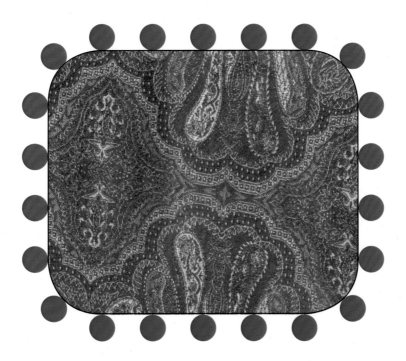

Laura Lee Washburn

A Story

Begins in a time and place
where the Earth begins
long ago west of the moon.
She is woebegone without mother
and he is woebegone
as a father doomed to marry.

What magic makes the man
reveal his daughter's grit?
She walks the soles through
three pair of iron shoes,
keeps every chicken's bones
in her sack. The stepmother
beats her, towers her,
mocks her in the ash. Father
marries her to the boar,
the stoat, ogre, genii,
murderer, handsome-one-
whose-mother-will-eat-
her-children, keeper of the keys.

When the story ends
and the century passes,
she has lost her shoes,
her hair, walked the Earth
from her father, been buried

to her neck, chopped up
and resurrected, made
beating a simple memory. She
holds her child to her breast,

takes from her sack
the chicken bones and climbs
their ladder until one wrung short
she chops off her little finger
to reach the door that ends
the story, breaks the evil,
makes wrong right, and so
they live happily until they die,
while the wicked end badly,
tied to a raging horse
which if he has not stopped
is running still.

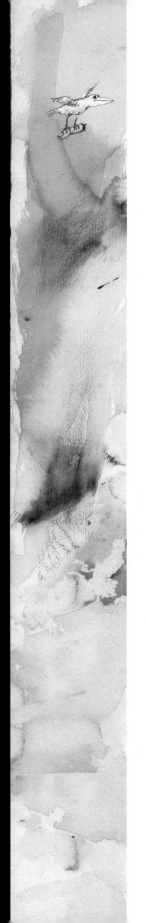

111

The Right Answer

for Josephine, raised without possibility

"There was no reply to her question and she did not expect one."
—P. L. Travers

I.

Climbing tall ladders they'd propped against the sky,
she watched the women paste gilt paper stars onto the air.

She had learned that tiny women with voices pitched
above whistles could break their fingers into sugar sticks;

that no amount of pampering, oysters, fresh cream, tartan
plaid overjackets, would make a small dog into a boy;

that even the vainest woman, one who checked her hat's roses
against the glistering shop window, could refuse, with a sniff, to speak;

that a steadfast chant and permanence of words feathered your ruff,
brought dove and pigeon warmth, the cooing nesting of your skirts;

that even Proper lives between hedges and the sky and dances
the sailor's hornpipe and the highland fling when it will and sees the
king;

that even dear mothers punish, the panda standing her fur on end,
the dolphin with her snout outthrust, the polar bear with fangs.

112

II.

Are the stars gold paper or is the gold paper stars?
Do fallen stars list on the horns of a cow?

The child in blue cloth ripped from sky, the second
of the Pleiades, walks invisible stairs back up to its home.

Your parents resist at least twenty-eight thousand visions
of the truth. They are like the cow who believed each dandelion
either sweet or sour, and not one moderately nice. But like any Jane
you'll read your books, and find the stars and paper
                             as good as gold or gingerbread.

Ana Merino

Adiós a la niñez

Adiós Peter Pan,
se aleja mi niñez
dando pasos de gigante
y tu sombra soy yo
convertida en mujer.

La tierra en donde vives
no me puede acoger
porque ahora sueño
que eres agua salada
mojándome la piel,
que eres un niño grande
bebiéndose mi sed.

Ya no puedo volar
porque mi boca
ha aprendido a morder
con dientes de deseo,
y he dejado de ser
la niña que encontraba
respuestas en los libros.
Ahora salgo a buscar
las piezas perdidas de mi alma
en los ojos cerrados de la noche.

En tu almohada

he guardado los tebeos
que leía de niña,
el pedazo de cielo de viñeta
que no podré alcanzar
por querer ser tu amante.

Adiós Peter Pan,
el eco de los niños
que no quieren crecer
y sólo juegan
me ha hecho recordar
que tuve sueños
que nunca jamás podrán cumplirse.

Good-Bye Childhood

by Ana Merino (Translated by Toshiya Kamei)

Good-bye Peter Pan,
my childhood walks away
with giant steps
and I'm your shadow
turned into a woman.

The land where you live
can't take me in
because now I dream
that you're saltwater
making my skin wet,
that you're a big boy
drinking my thirst.

I can't fly anymore
because my mouth
has learned to bite
with teeth of desire,
and I'm no longer
the girl who found
answers in books.
Now I go look for
lost pieces of my soul
in the closed eyes of night.

Under your pillow
I've kept comics
that I read as a girl,
a piece of the vignette sky
I can't reach
for wanting to be your lover.

Good-bye Peter Pan,
the echo of children
who don't want to grow up
and only play
has reminded me
that I had dreams
that will never come true.

Teddybear by Hanna Landgrebe

El genio Garabato

Cuando la Tierra era plana
y los desiertos tan grandes como el cielo,
si la tristeza acechaba
podías buscar consuelo
en el bazar de Damasco,
donde un viejo comerciante
vendía miles de frascos
que guardaban las esencias
de los olores más finos
o los sabores más raros.

Cuando la Tierra era plana
y las culebras de mar eran dragones,
en el bazar de Damasco
solía dormir un gato
conocido como el genio Garabato.

Allí pasaba las horas
dentro de un frasco verdoso
que guardaba los aceites
que curan a los leprosos.

Olía a mirra y a eneldo,
bostezaba todo el tiempo
porque el calor le agotaba
y el pobre se evaporaba
con el sol de los desiertos.

Era un genio bondadoso,
lleno de sabiduría,
pero solo poseía
poder para realizar
un deseo sobrehumano.

Cuando la Tierra era plana,
pasaron muchos viajeros
por el bazar de Damasco
y anotaron sus deseos
en un pergamino viejo,
mientras compraban los frascos
de aceites llenos de hinojo,
de eucalipto o de naranja,
para curar el cansancio
o las dolencias extrañas.

Aquel genio se aburría
leyendo todos los días
las cosas que le pedían
peregrinos y viajeros,
porque siempre deseaban
poseer grandes riquezas
y todos se repetían
pidiendo oro y diamantes
y otras joyas elegantes,
creyendo que las fortunas
les harían importantes.

Cuando la Tierra era plana,
sucedió lo inesperado,
hubo un deseo curioso

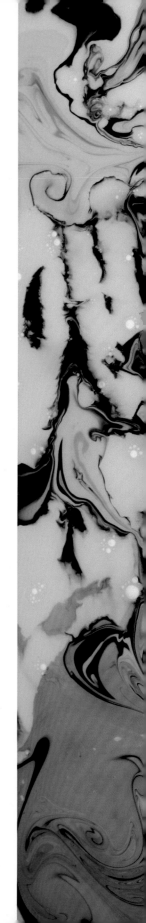

119

que hizo que Garabato
se sintiera poderoso.

Cuando la Tierra era plana,
un niño le pidió al gato
que el mundo no fuese plano.
Así el genio Garabato
hizo la Tierra planeta
y la convirtió en esfera.

Teddybear by Steven Gordon

Doodle the Genie

by Ana Merino (Translated by Toshiya Kamei)

When the Earth was flat
and the deserts as big as the sky
if sadness awaited you
you could look for comfort
in the bazaar of Damascus
where an old trader
sold thousands of bottles
filled with the essences
of the finest smells
or the rarest flavors.

When the earth was flat
and sea snakes were dragons
in the bazaar of Damascus
there slept a cat
named Doodle the Genie.

There he spent hours
inside a greenish bottle
filled with oil
that cures lepers.

He smelled myrrh and dill
and yawned all the time
because the heat tired him out
and the poor cat evaporated
with the desert sun.

He was a kind genie
full of wisdom,
but only he had
the power to make
wishes come true.

When the Earth was flat,
many travelers came
to the bazaar of Damascus
and wrote down their wishes
on an ancient scroll
while they bought the bottles
of oils full of fennel
of eucalyptus or of orange
to cure exhaustion
or strange ailments.

The genie was bored
reading day after day
the wishes pilgrims
and travelers made
because they always wanted
great wealth
and everyone asked for
gold and diamonds
and other elegant jewelry,
believing that their fortunes
would make them important.

When the Earth was flat
the unexpected happened.
Doodle found a curious wish

122

that made him
feel powerful.

When the Earth was flat
a boy wished
the world weren't flat.
So Doodle the Genie
made the Earth a planet
and turned it into a sphere.

Angelia Northrip-Rivera

Alice in the Carnival Square: Reading Carroll Through a Bakhtinian Looking-Glass

Charles Lutwidge Dodgson (1832-1898) was an Oxford don of mathematics, a clergyman, and an obsessive manager of every small detail of his life. A Victorian of the first water, Dodgson's personal predilection for propriety and order mirrored that of his society. As a mathematician, he was conservative and logical; as a man, he was compulsively organized, going so far as to catalog his vast correspondence and keep records of seating plans of his many dinner parties; as a writer, he kept a tight control on every aspect of the publishing of his books, from typesetting to the tiniest details of illustration. Dodgson published mathematical treatises, such as *Euclid and His Modern Rivals* (1885) and "Infinities and Infinitudes" (1893), as well as logical explorations, such as *Principles of Parliamentary Representation* (1885), and he was a very good amateur photographer, setting up elaborately staged and posed tableaux to create exactly the effects he wanted. Dodgson kept himself and the manageable details of his life and work restrained—nothing that could be controlled was left to chance, and those things that could not be controlled were avoided. Life was a serious reality.

Lewis Carroll (1832-1898) was a writer of children's books. His two best-known works are *Alice's Adventures in Wonderland* (1865) and *Through the Looking-Glass, and What Alice Found There* (1872). Later works included *The Hunting of the Snark* (1876), *Sylvie and Bruno* (1889), and *Sylvie and Bruno Concluded* (1893). Carroll's work is chiefly described as nonsense—amusing stories and poems written to be read by children for fun. He said that the writing was unplanned, and that his two most famous books were "made up almost wholly of bits and scraps, single ideas which came of themselves" (Carroll, "Alice on" 281). Carroll loved children; in fact, the *Alice* books began as stories told to three young sisters during long boat rides in the summer of 1862. He often entertained children at tea parties in his rooms at Christ Church and wrote them amusing letters when they were away from him. For Carroll, life was a joyous dream.

Lewis Carroll was the pen name of Charles Lutwidge Dodgson. This complex man with the strikingly dual nature was the author of both dry and logical mathematical tomes and fanciful nonsense verse. It is little wonder, then, that this doubleness in life led to a similar doubleness in art. Carroll/Dodgson was a human counterpart to Mikhail Bakhtin's words about the novels of Fyodor Dostoevsky, since Carroll had "[a] stubborn urge to see everything as co-existing, to perceive and show all things side by side and simultaneous … even internal contradictions and internal stages in the development of a single person—forcing a character to converse with his own double" (Bakhtin, *Problems* 28). In some forms of his writings, he combined these two seemingly irreconcilable elements into a most original Carrollinian carnivalesque hybrid. For instance, in a short essay entitled "What the Tortoise Said to Achilles," Carroll combined the explanation by a tortoise of Euclid's First Proposition with tangential jokes and plays on words; in "The New Method of Evaluation as Applied to π," the punning epigraph reads, "Little Jack Horner / sat in a corner / eating his Christmas pie" (*Complete* 1011). However, carnivalesque elements are most evident in his two finest works—products more of the Carroll side of his nature—*Alice's Adventures in Wonderland* (*Wonderland* hereafter) and *Through the Looking-Glass* (*Looking-Glass* hereafter). Through the Victorian trappings of the Alice books, the reader hears the laughter of carnival where images are "ambivalent" and "dualistic" (Bakhtin, *Problems* 126).

One of the most evident elements of the carnivalesque can be found in Carroll's parodying of the didactic poetry that children of the Victorian Age were expected to memorize and recite. The first such parody in *Won-*

125

derland is of an Isaac Watts poem entitled "Against Idleness and Mischief."
Watts's original reads as follows:

> How doth the little busy bee
>   improve each shining hour,
> and gather honey all the day
>   from every opening flower!
>
> How skillfully she builds her cell!
>   How neat she spreads the wax!
> And labours hard to store it well
>   with the sweet food she makes.
>
> In works of labour or of skill,
>   I would be busy too;
> for Satan finds some mischief still
>   for idle hands to do.
>
> In books, or work, or healthful play,
>   let my first years be past,
> that I may give for every day
>   some good account at last. (Carroll, *Alice's Adventures* 16, note)

Alice uses this poem as a method of determining her identity in Wonderland. She has been through the rabbit hole, has changed size several
times by eating and drinking Wonderland food and drink, and has lost
her sense of self: "Who in the world am I? Ah, that's the great puzzle!"
(15). She wonders if she has become one of the other children she knows,
and she sets herself a test to see "if I still know all the things I used to
know" as a means of determining who she is (16). She decides to recite
"How Doth the Little Busy Bee," a poem she knows, but "the words did
not come the same as they used to do":

126

How doth the little crocodile
    improve his shining tail,
and pour the waters of the Nile
    on every golden scale!

How cheerfully he seems to grin,
    how neatly spreads his claws,
and welcomes little fishes in,
    with gently smiling jaws! (16)

Comparisons between the two versions of the poem show the "carnival-ization of speech" (Bakhtin, *Rabelais* 426) introduced by Carroll. The first element is the parody of style. Rhyme scheme and meter are the same between the two verses, as if, like a parodied song, they could be "sung" to the same tune. As a second element of carnivalization, he takes an in-structive poem for children of Victorian society and subverts its message. Rather than praising the industriousness of the bee, the second poem tells, in poetic language, of the self-centered crocodile who improves himself and anoints his own body with river water. The "smiling" croco-dile deals death to the "little fishes," whereas the "busy" bee preserves life by storing food. Carroll chooses to parody only the first two stanzas of the poem, possibly from a wish to avoid mocking religion, but even with-out the last two stanzas, Carroll's subversion of the theme is complete.[1] On parody, Bakhtin writes,

> [T]he author … speaks in someone else's discourse [… and] in-troduces into that discourse a semantic intention that is directly opposed to the original one. The second voice, once having made its home in the other's discourse, clashes hostilely with its primordial host and forces him to serve directly opposing aims. Discourse becomes an arena of battle between two voices. (*Problems* 193)

Because Watts's poem was general knowledge in Carroll's England at the time of his writing, the two competing voices were very evident to readers of the parodied poem. Though we now need footnotes to compare the two, Victorians knew and recognized the parody for what it was—a jab at the moral nursery teachings that children of the time were accustomed to hearing. Carroll is "uncrowning" the moral literature of the nursery, and is introducing carnivalistic elements into a previously unrelievedly serious subject (Bakhtin, *Rabelais* 305).

Another example of poetic parody in *Wonderland* can be found in Carroll's version of "The Old Man's Comforts and How He Gained Them," by Robert Southey. Again, this poem is used by Alice to help her determine the answer to the question, "Who are you?" (asked this time by a hookah-smoking Caterpillar). The last two stanzas of Southey's poem give the gist of its message:

> "You are old Father William," the young man cried,
>   "and life must be hastening away;
> You are cheerful, and love to converse upon death:
>   Now tell me the reason, I pray."
>
> "I am cheerful young man," Father William replied;
>   "let the cause thy attention engage:
> In the days of my youth, I remembered my God:
> And he hath not forgotten my age." (Carroll, *Alice's Adventures* 36, note)

Southey's poem, like Watts's, was a popular and well-known set piece for recitation. Carroll stands the sentiment (and the old man) on its ear with his carnivalistic parody. I quote the entire poem, as elements from each stanza will be important to this argument:

> "You are old Father William," the young man said,
>   "and your hair has become very white;

128

and yet you incessantly stand on your head—
    do you think, at your age, it is right?"

"In my youth," Father William replied to his son,
    "I feared it might injure the brain;
but, now that I'm perfectly sure I have none,
    why, I do it again and again."

"You are old," said the youth, "as I mentioned before,
    and have grown most uncommonly fat;
yet you turned a back-somersault in at the door—
    pray, what is the reason of that?"

"In my youth," said the sage, as he shook his gray locks,
    "I kept my limbs very supple
by the use of this ointment—one shilling the box—
    allow me to sell you a couple?"

"You are old," said the youth, "and your jaws are too weak
    for anything tougher than suet;
yet you finished the goose, with the bones and the beak—
    pray, how did you manage to do it?"

"In my youth," said his father, "I took to the law,
    and argued each case with my wife;
and the muscular strength, which it gave to my jaw
    has lasted the rest of my life."

"You are old," said the youth, "one would hardly suppose
    that your eye was as steady as ever;
yet you balanced an eel on the end of your nose—
    what made you so awfully clever?"

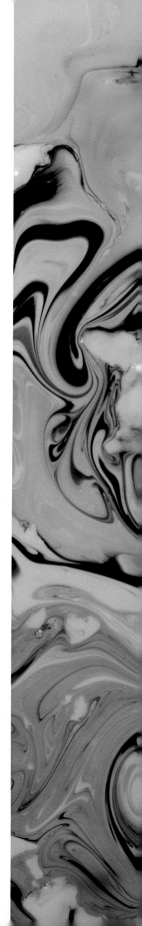

129

"I have answered three questions, and that is enough,"
　　said his father. "Don't give yourself airs!
Do you think I can listen all day to such stuff?
　　Be off, or I'll kick you downstairs!" (Carroll, *Wonderland* 37-40)

Once again, Carroll imitates the meter and rhyme scheme of Southey's original, but the original meaning and overtones of piousness have given way to carnival laughter.

The central character of the poem, Father William, is a form of the Seventeenth-Century character Gros Guillame (Fat William), "one of the most popular figures of comic folklore" (Bakhtin, *Rabelais* 292). The fat body (especially the belly) of the character symbolized the "abundance of earthly goods" and demonstrated what Bakhtin calls the "grotesque image of the body" that is such an important carnivalesque element (292).

In the first stanza, the old man stands on his head. In *Rabelais and His World,* Bakhtin writes of the

> downward movement … inherent in all forms of popular-festive merriment and grotesque realism. Down, inside out, vice versa, upside down, such is the direction of all these movements. All of them thrust down, turn over, push headfirst, transfer top to bottom, and bottom to top, both in the literal sense of space, and in the metaphorical meaning of the image. (370)

Another literal instance of this upside-down, backward movement is evident in the second dialogue of the poem by the "back-somersaults" the old man uses to come through the door. He arrives inverted top to bottom as the result of a backwards motion and presents himself upside-down to the person who opens the door—a complete reversal of convention. The "metaphorical meaning of the image" can be seen in its use (Bakhtin, *Rabelais* 370). This poem turns upside-down and backward the moral tone of Southey's original. Instead of espousing piousness, the parody renders nonsensical the lesson of its referent.

The carnival image of feasting is evident in this poem as well. Bakhtin writes of the grotesque body that

> The distinctive character of this body is its open unfinished nature, its interaction with the world. These traits are most fully and concretely revealed in the act of eating: the body transgresses here its own limits: it swallows, devours, rends the world apart, is enriched, and grows at the world's expense. The encounter of man with the world, which takes place inside the open, biting, rending, chewing mouth, is one of the most important objects of human thought and imagery. (*Rabelais* 281)

Compare this devouring, rending mouth to the lines in the third dialogue between the youth and Father William. The young man maintains that though Father William is old, he has managed to eat a goose, "with the bones and the beak" (Carroll, *Alice's Adventures* 39). Here we have a clear picture of the grotesque body. In *Rabelais and His World,* Bakhtin gives an example in which he says, "[T]he limits between animal flesh and the consuming human flesh are dimmed…. The bodies are interwoven and begin to be fused" (221). Bakhtin's illustration is of Gargamelle, whose overindulgence in tripe (beef intestines) causes her own intestines to drop out of her body. Compare this example to that of Father William, who is able to consume the beak (mouth) and the bones of the goose, because his mouth and his jaw (a bone) have been strengthened by his legal arguments before his wife. Here the barriers between the human and animal bodies are surely "dimmed" and "interwoven" (221); the body is "transgressing its own limits" (281), and as such, is an example of the carnivalization of the body in Carroll's poem. This idea of consuming in order to create can also be applied to the very idea of parody itself. The parodic poet "devours" and "rends," cannibalizing the original poet (and his/her poem) to create his own.

In the final dialogue of Carroll's parody, we find the old man physically threatening the youth. Father William says, "I have answered three questions, and that is enough" and "Don't give yourself airs" (Carroll, *Wonderland* 40). This warning to the youth seems to be against his giving himself authority—crowning himself, as it were. Father William threatens to "kick [him] down-stairs"(40); that is, he will uncrown the youth. Bakhtin writes, "Here is a dimension in which chastisement and abuse are not a personal chastisement but are the symbolic actions directed at something on a higher level" (Bakhtin, *Rabelais* 197). The old man is rebelling not against the youth, but against any authority that believes itself to be capable of controlling his time and energy. According to Bakhtin, carnival "mark[s] the suspension of all hierarchical rank, privileges, norms, and prohibitions" (10), and this final dialogue of the poem is a clear illustration of the applicability of the term *carnival* to Carroll's parody of Southey's poem.

This rebellion and overturning of authority is another important element of the carnivalesque found in Carroll's books. Though we see a hint of it in the poem previously discussed, other examples are abundant and can be found in both *Wonderland* and *Looking-Glass.*

Perhaps one of the most well known characters from *Alice in Wonderland* is the Queen of Hearts, whose almost constant refrain of "Off with her head" (or "his head" or "their heads") echoes through the final four chapters of Carroll's book. In this character, we can see an image of royalty crowned and ultimately uncrowned, for, though Alice greets her with a very proper, "My name is Alice, so please your Majesty," she is thinking, at the same time, "Why they're only a pack of cards, after all. I needn't be afraid of them" (Carroll, *Alice's Adventure* 63).[2] As Bakhtin writes, "From the very beginning, a decrowning glimmers through the crowning" (*Problems* 125). Alice, a child, is able to triumph over a Queen in the tale because she refuses to grant to the Queen the authority to rule. At every turn, Alice's carnivalistic liberty thwarts the Queen's attempts to dominate her. For example, when Alice answers one of the Queen's questions with the retort,

132

"How should I know…? It's no business of mine." The Queen turned crimson with fury, and, after glaring at [Alice] for a moment like a wild beast, began screaming "Off with her head! Off with—"

"Nonsense!" said Alice, very loudly and decidedly, and the Queen was silent. (Carroll, *Wonderland* 64)

As a child in Victorian England, Alice had no power in society; she was completely dependent upon and subject to the adults around her. In Wonderland, she experiences what Bakhtin calls "free and familiar contact" (*Problems* 123). He goes on to write,

This is a very important aspect of a carnival sense of the world. People who in life are separated by impenetrable hierarchical barriers enter into free and familiar contact on the carnival square. … The behavior, gesture, and discourse of a person are freed from the authority of all hierarchical positions (social, estate, rank, age, property) defining them totally in noncarnival life, and thus from the vantage point of noncarnival life become eccentric and inappropriate. (123)

Thus, in the carnival square of Wonderland, Alice is able to countermand the Queen's orders, shout at her, and laugh at her discomfiture when the White Rabbit tells Alice that the Duchess "boxed the Queen's ears," a remark which causes Alice to give "a little scream of laughter" (*Wonderland* 65).

If *Wonderland* gives an illustration of the overthrow of royalty, *Looking-Glass* turns the hierarchy of knowledge upon its head. Humpty Dumpty has been described by George Shelden Hubbell as "the professor in an eggshell" (191), and, as a character, he is the essence of what Bakhtin calls the "carnivalization of speech … a form which granted momentary liberation from all logical links" (Bakhtin, *Rabelais* 426). He uses words in eccentric ways:

133

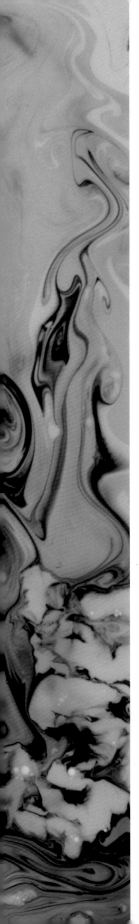

> "When I use a word," Humpty Dumpty said, in a rather scornful
> tone, "it means just what I choose it to mean—neither more nor
> less."
>
> "The question is," said Alice, "whether you can make words
> mean so many different things."
>
> "The question is," said Humpty Dumpty, "which is to be mas-
> ter—that's all." (Carroll, *Through* 163)

With this passage, Carroll subverts the idea of a single body of knowledge
to be gained. If words have personal, illogical, and arbitrary meanings,
then knowledge is a vain pursuit; those who are in authority by virtue of
their learning will be decrowned by the carnival laughter of the people.
In Looking-Glass Land—Carroll's carnival—nothing can be known as a
certainty, because the essence of carnival is uncertainty—things are not
as they seem.

With Carroll's comic parody and overturning of authority comes a
third type of carnivalistic element in his books—the use of carnival objects. Two good examples of these are found in *Looking-Glass:* the battle
between the twins Tweedledee and Tweedledum and the inventions and
other belongings of the White Knight.

Tweedledee and Tweedledum are carnivalistic figures in their own
rights. Opposites, whose favorite word is "contrariwise," they illustrate
the carnivalistic duality which Bakhtin writes is "very characteristic for
carnival thinking ... paired images chosen for their contrast ... or for
their similarity (doubles/twins). Also characteristic is the utilization of
things in reverse: ... dishes in place of headgear, the use of household
utensils as weapons" (Bakhtin, *Problems* 126). While Alice is with the
Tweedles, they stage an elaborate battle for which she is called upon to
help them dress in things "such as bolsters, blankets, hearth-rugs, ta-
ble-cloths, dish-covers, and coal scuttles," a carnivalistic battle-armor
complete with saucepan helmets (Carroll, *Through* 147). This scene par-
allels Bakhtin's writing of "carnival objects. They are, so to speak, turned

134

inside-out, utilized in the wrong way, contrary to their common use. Household objects are turned into arms" (*Rabelais* 411). As Tweedledum tells his brother, "There's only one sword, you know ... but you can have the umbrella—it's quite as sharp" (Carroll, *Through* 148).

Another carnivalistic figure of *Looking-Glass* is the White Knight. He is supposed to be Alice's protector, but for much of the time that she is with him, he is falling off his horse. This military figure is, paradoxically (or should I say carnivalistically), the gentlest character in the book. He travels on a horse heavily laden with his inventions and other baggage. The horse wears a bell on his forehead, an interesting parallel to the story of Gargantua, who stole cathedral bells to hang on his horse. Bakhtin writes, "Uncrowning the cathedral bells and hanging them on a horse is a typical carnivalesque gesture of debasement" (*Rabelais* 214). Though the cathedral is absent in *Looking-Glass,* the bell on the horse's forehead does show up later as the doorbell to a royal palace; the debasement in this example is not of the Church, but of royalty.

The Knight's inventions are carnivalesque objects. He invents a small box to hang on his back:

> " ... to keep clothes and sandwiches in. You see, I carry it up-side-down, so that the rain ca'n't get in."
>
> "But the things can get out," Alice gently remarked. "Do you know the lid's open?"
>
> "I didn't know it," the Knight said.... "Then all of the things must have fallen out! And the box is no use without them." He unfastened it as he spoke, and was just going to throw it into the bushes, when a sudden thought seemed to strike him, and he hung it carefully on a tree. "Can you guess why I did that?" he said to Alice.
>
> Alice shook her head.
>
> "In hopes some bees may make a nest in it—then I should get the honey." (Carroll, *Through* 181)

Once again, objects are used for purposes for which they were not designed. In a carnivalistic turn, a failure is turned into an opportunity—the invention is reinvented. Bakhtin writes, "The object that has been destroyed remains in the world but in a new form of being in time and space; it becomes the 'other side' of the new object that has taken its place" (*Rabelais* 410).

Also evident in the episode of Alice and the White Knight is the downward motion that I addressed earlier in regard to Father William. During the conversation between Alice and the Knight he falls off his horse, headfirst into a ditch. She finds him unhurt, but upside-down:

> "How can you go on talking so quietly, head downwards?" Alice asked, as she dragged him out by the feet, and laid him in a heap on the bank.
>
> The Knight looked surprised at the question. "What does it matter where my body happens to be?" he said. "My mind goes on working just the same. In fact, the more head-downwards I am, the more I keep inventing new things." (Carroll, *Through* 185-6)

The Knight benefits from the carnivalistic overturning; Bakhtin writes that "we … see the downward movement in fights, beatings, and blows [and falls?]; they throw the adversary to the ground, trample him into the earth…. But at the same time they are creative" (*Rabelais* 370). The Knight is more creative precisely because he is upside-down in the carnival world beyond the Looking-Glass; by being thrown down to the earth, he is "regenerated" (435).

How is it possible that Carroll, with his Victorian sensibilities, was able to conceive and produce such carnivalesque works? Bakhtin addresses this point when writing about Dostoevsky:

> Carnivalization acted on him, as on the majority of other Eigh-teen-and Nineteenth-Century writers, primarily as a literary

136

and generic tradition whose extraliterary source, that is, carnival proper, was perhaps not even perceived by him in any clearly precise way.... In order to master this language, that is, to attach himself to the carnivalistic generic tradition in literature, a writer need not know all the links and all the branching of that tradition." (*Problems* 157)

Carroll was influenced by the literature of writers who were influenced by carnival, but I believe another source was more important to his work. Carroll loved children—those most carnivalesque of humans. Children delight in the upside-down, the triumph of the underdog, the pricking of balloons, noise, eating and drinking—they appreciate and seek out the freedom of carnival. Robert Polhemus calls Carroll "the don of comic reduction: shrink the essence of authority to a child's scale, diminish the threatening urgencies of society, make fun of them, show up their triviality—those are his imperatives" (367). The child's imagination and delight is at the heart of Carroll's writing; he wrote the books, not for an adult audience, but for Alice Liddell, a child he loved. These books, shaped through their telling as rambling stories on long summer afternoons, are masterpieces of nonsense—of the carnivalesque, of childlike imagination.

Carroll once wrote, "I'm very much afraid I didn't mean anything but nonsense! Still, you know, words mean more than we mean to express when we use them; so a whole book ought to mean a great deal more than the writer meant" (qtd. in Stern 141). This seems, with the following words of Bakhtin, to sum up the reasons for the continued success of the strange, but wonderful, books of a strangely divided, but brilliant, writer: "Thanks to the intentional potential embedded in them, such works have proved capable of uncovering in each era and against ever new dialogizing backgrounds ever newer aspects of meaning; their semantic content literally continues to grow, to further create out of itself" (Bakhtin, *Dialogic* 421). Words do, you know, mean more than we think or expect. The enduring charm and timeless images in the words of Charles Lutwidge Dodgson/Lewis Carroll are ample proof of that.

Notes

[1] In a letter to a friend about the relationship between laughter and religious thought, Carroll once wrote, "While the laughter or joy is in full harmony with our deeper life, the laughter of amusement should be kept apart from it. The danger is too great of thus learning to look at solemn things in a spirit of mockery, and to seek in them opportunities for exercising wit" (Carroll, *Letters* 317).

[2] The introduction of playing cards into the story is, in itself, a carnivalesque image. Bakhtin writes that "It [the carnival image] strives to encompass and unite within itself both poles of becoming or both members of an antithesis ... while the upper pole of a two-in-one image is reflected in the lower, after the manner of the figures on playing cards" (*Problems* 176). *In Rabelais and his World,* Bakhtin writes of "games ... as a condensed formula of life and of the historic process.... Figures in card games represented world events ... chessmen are represented as real people, wearing conventional costumes inspired by that game" (235). *Through the Looking-Glass* uses a chess game as its central motif.

Works Cited

Bakhtin, Mikhail. *The Dialogic Imagination: Four Essays by M.M. Bakhtin.* Ed. Michael Holquist. Trans. Caryl Emerson and Michael Holquist. Austin, TX: U of Texas P, 1981. Print.

——. *Problems of Dostoevsky's Poetics.* Ed. and Trans. Caryl Emerson. Minneapolis, MN: U of Minnesota P, 1984. Print.

——. *Rabelais and His World.* Trans. Hélène Iswolsky. Bloomington, IN: Indiana UP, 1984. Print.

Carroll, Lewis. *Alice in Wonderland.* Ed. Donald J. Gray. Second Norton Critical Edition. NY: Norton, 1992. Print.

——. "Alice on the Stage." *The Theatre* 9.52 (April 1887): 179-184. Print.

——. *Alice's Adventures in Wonderland.* 1897. *Alice in Wonderland.* Second Norton Critical Edition. Ed. Donald J. Gray. New York: Norton, 1992. Print.

——. *The Complete Works of Lewis Carroll.* NY: Barnes & Noble, Inc., 1994. Print.

——. *Letters. Alice in Wonderland.* Second Norton Critical Edition. Ed. Donald J. Gray. NY: Norton, 1992. Print.

——. *Through the Looking-Glass, and What Alice Found There.* 1872.

Hubbell, George Sheldon. "Triple Alice." *Sewanee Review* 48 (1940): 174-195. Print.

Polhemous, Robert. "The Comedy of Regression." *Alice in Wonderland.* Ed. Donald J. Gray. Second Norton Critical Edition. New York: Norton, 1992. Print.

Sterne, Jeffrey. "Lewis Carroll the Surrealist." *Lewis Carroll: A Celebration.* Ed. Edward Guiliano. New York: Clarkson N. Potter, Inc., 1982. 132-153. Print.

James S. Baumlin and Hercule Pervukhinoid

"Derelicts": Some Visual Remembrances
of *Treasure Island*

In 1882, Scottish novelist Robert Louis Stevenson published his children's
novel, *Treasure Island.* On the run from his pirate mates, "Cap'n Billy
Bones" enters a seaside inn, bearing a sea chest and repeating the snippet
of a shanty:

> Fifteen men on a dead man's chest—
> 　　Yo-ho-ho and a bottle of rum!
> Drink and the devil had done for the rest—
> 　　Yo-ho-ho and a bottle of rum!

It's his own life that Billy sings, and he's trapped within its terms for the
time that is left to him. Found out by his old mates, Billy fights and dies
in the inn. And Jim Hawkins, the novel's young narrator, opens the dead
man's chest to find a treasure map. The rest, as they say, is adventure on
the high seas, as the boy sails off in search of pirate gold.

Stevenson invented this fragment of a sea-shanty, which flaunts the
pirate's two insatiable thirsts: gold and rum. Stevenson was aware of the
Caribbean "Dead Chest Island," where Blackbeard (so the legend goes)
marooned some insubordinates. Possibly, Stevenson alters the island's
name to make it a clue, from Billy's own mouth, as to where the full
treasure lies. (The novel never tells.) But the general reader, then as now,
would tend to literalize the reference, since sailors used sea chests for
their clothing and gear and, whether earned or stolen, gold.

Read in this latter sense, Billy's shanty predicts carnage, as we are to
imagine men standing "on" or over a "dead man's chest," greed urging
each toward more than his share. After fighting, they'll soon be laying

140

"on" the chest themselves, murdered by their own greed. For "the rest" of the pirate crew, "drink and the devil" has already doomed or "done" them in. And yet Billy Bones does not heed his own song's message: having gone into hiding, Billy hoards his treasure—the greatest piece being the map, not the gold beneath it—all the while drowning himself in drink.

Stevenson's novel fired the imaginations of readers young and old, for whom adventurous freedom remained an alluring fantasy-alternative to the humdrum of daily, rule-bound routine. In 1891, American news-paperman Young E. Allison (1853-1932) wrote "Derelict," subtitled "A Reminiscence of 'Treasure Island,'" which he published in the Louisville *Courier-Journal.* Allison's poem has little to do with Stevenson's novel; instead, it places Billy's refrain within a larger narrative of pirate mutiny.

Allison's unnamed speaker begins with a harrowing sight—fifteen men murdered—though we assume he's just boarded and is piecing together the "derelict" or abandoned ship's mysteries. "There they lay," the speak-er notes, "Like break o'day in a boozing ken"—like a pile of drunkards sleeping it off outside a tavern. But theirs is the sleep of death. A sprin-kling of nautical terms (current in Allison's day, largely forgotten now) adds to the ambience, but mystery remains Allison's focus: not how, but why these men died. Below decks, the speaker and his fellows find loads of Spanish loot. In the penultimate stanza (italicized for emphasis) the speaker finds that a woman, stowed in the captain's quarters, had died. (*Did she share in or cause the mutiny?*) In the end, the "yo-ho-ho" turns from a drinking song to a worker's shanty—*a yo-heave-ho!*—as the ship's new crew swings the bodies overboard, burying them at sea.

The ship belongs now to the unnamed speaker and his crew-com-panions; and they—unlike the pirates, who lose all for wanting all—will share the booty "by rule of thumb," that is, more or less equally. But … has the new crew broken already into the rum locker? Will they keep to this "rule of thumb"? Or are they, too, doomed to drink, and fight, and die, all for pirate gold?

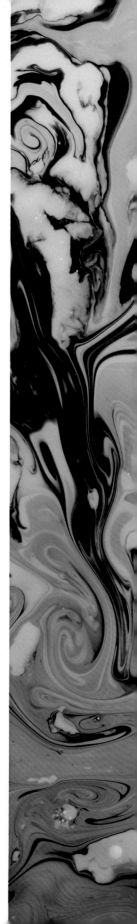

So goes Allison's poem. Now it's time for Allison to enjoy his own poem-inspired series of "reminiscences." Following his pirate-poem, we present four contemporary images by graphic artists Stephenie Walker, Tim Korychuck, and Frank Norton, Jr., each responding to a poetic line or theme. These images represent a recent (and growing) movement in graphic illustration, one that reconfigures children's literature as adult literature, replacing conventional designs with darker, more ambivalent images intended for adult consumption.

Fifteen men on a dead man's chest—
    Yo-ho-ho and a bottle of rum!
Drink and the devil had done for the rest—
    Yo-ho-ho and a bottle of rum!
The mate was fixed by the bosun's pike,
The bosun brained with a marlinspike,
And cookey's throat was marked belike
      It had been gripped
        By fingers ten;
    And there they lay,
      All good dead men,
Like break o'day in a boozing ken—
Yo-ho-ho and a bottle of rum!

Fifteen men of the whole ship's list—
    Yo-ho-ho and a bottle of rum!
Dead and be damned and the rest gone whist—
    Yo-ho-ho and a bottle of rum!
The skipper lay with his nob in gore
Where the scullion's axe his cheek had shore—
And the scullion he was stabbed times four
      And there they lay,
      And the soggy skies

Three wise men of Gotham

Went to sea in a bowl;

If the bowl had been stronger,

My story would have been longer.

Illustration by Frank Norton, Jr.

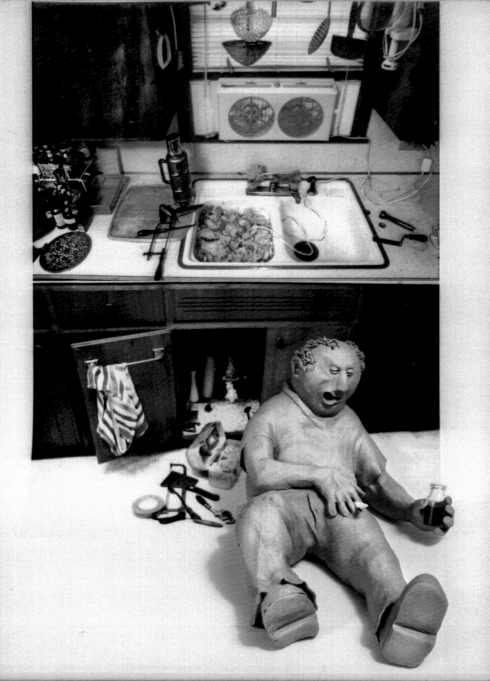

Dripped all day long
    In up-staring eyes—
At murk sunset and at foul sunrise—
    Yo-ho-ho and a bottle of rum!

Fifteen men of 'em stiff and stark—
    Yo-ho-ho and a bottle of rum!
Ten of the crew had the murder mark—
    Yo-ho-ho and a bottle of rum!
'Twas a cutlass swipe or an ounce of lead
Or a yawing hole in a battered head—
And the scuppers' glut with a rotting red.
    And there they lay,
      Aye, damn my eyes! —
    Looking up at paradise—
      All souls bound just contrariwise—
    Yo-ho-ho and a bottle of rum!

Fifteen men of 'em good and true—
    Yo-ho-ho and a bottle of rum!
Ev'ry man jack could ha' sailed with Old Pew—
    Yo-ho-ho and a bottle of rum!
There was chest on chest of Spanish gold,
With a ton of plate in the middle hold,
And the cabins riot of stuff untold.
    And they lay there
      That took the plum,
    With sightless glare
      And their lips struck dumb,
While we shared all by the rule of thumb—
    Yo-ho-ho and a bottle of rum!

More was seen through a sternlight screen—
  Yo-ho-ho and a bottle of rum!
Chartings undoubt where a woman had been!
  Yo-ho-ho and a bottle of rum!
'Twas a flimsy shift on a bunker cot,
With a dirk slit sheer through the bosom spot
And the lace stiff dry in a purplish blot
    Or was she wench …
      Or some shudderin' maid …
That dared the knife and took the blade!
By God! She was stuff for a plucky jade—
  Yo-ho-ho and a bottle of rum!

Fifteen men on a dead man's chest—
Yo-ho-ho and a bottle of rum!
Drink and the devil had done for the rest—
Yo-ho-ho and a bottle of rum!
We wrapped 'em all in a mains'l tight
With twice ten turns of a hawser's bight,
And we heaved 'em over and out of sight,
    With a yo-heave-ho!
      And a fare-you-well!
    And a sudden plunge
      In the sullen swell
Ten fathoms deep on the road to hell!
  Yo-ho-ho and a bottle of rum!

146

Treasure *Island*

written by
Ken Ludwig

Starring

Skyler Holman as Jim Hawkins
Jeff Robinson as Captain Smollett
Tim Curry as Long John Silver
Greg Barnett as Blind Pew

David Stensrud as Billy Bones
Ryan Poole as Captain Flint
Eric Armstrong as Dr. Livesey
Jeck Dickamore as Israel Hands

Act One
Shiver My Timbers
Something Better
We're Gonna Be Rich!

Act Two
Sailing for Adventure
Cabin Fever
Land!

Act Three
Professional Pirates
Boom Shakalaka
Love Led Us HEre

Illustration by Stephenie Walker

IV. Songs of Experience

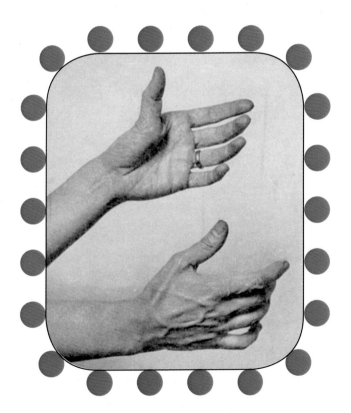

VI

Jacek Frączak

Sztuka i Dziecko

W pierwszym rozdziale swej sławnej i prowokacyjnej książki pod tytułem „Koniec Sztuki", jej autor, nowojorski krytyk i profesor historii sztuki w Szkole Sztuk Wizualnych, profesor Donald Kuspit przytoczył i skomentował opinię, jaką ongiś wygłosił wielki malarz, nestor amerykańskiej sztuki nowoczesnej, Frank Stella, na temat głośnej wystawy pt. „Początki Nowoczesności" otwartej w MoMa w 2001 roku i opracowanej przez kuratora Johna Elderfielda. Była to opinia bardzo krytyczna, by nie rzec druzgocąca dla samej wystawy, ale też i stawiająca radykalną diagnozę co do miejsca współczesnej sztuki w społeczeństwie. Stary Mistrz w mocnych słowach krytykuje miałkość obecnej sztuki, martwi go łatwość z jaką przystała na błahą rolę masowej rozrywki bądź swoiście poważną rolę – stricte komercyjnego obiektu. Kuspit podkreśla, że dla Stelli we współczesnych praktykach artystycznych zatraceniu uległo kluczowe dla dotychczasowego pojmowania sztuki pojęcie przeżycia estetycznego. Tego wyjątkowego stanu, który nie jest ze swej istoty demokratyczny, ma charakter chwilowego 'objawienia', 'metafizycznej rewelacji' i ukojenia wobec banalności życia i cierpień przez nie niesionych. Ten stan chwilo-

151

wego, intensywnego przeżywania świata i siebie w nim, stan pozytywnej fascynacji wywołanej kontaktem z dziełem sztuki Stella i Kuspit porównują z postawą dziecka i stanem dzieciństwa jako najczystszym stanem twórczego i wrażliwego przeżywania świata.

Jest sporo moich prac, w których albo bezpośrednio przywołuję postaci dzieci, albo staram się stworzyć obrazy nasycone ekscytacją światem, tą rewelacją jaką pamiętam z czasów własnego dzieciństwa. Mogą to być konkretne miejsca sportretowane bezpośrednio, ale częściej jakoś przetworzone na miarę ofiarowanej mi przez nie magii. Ponieważ praktykę artystyczną rozpocząłem względnie wcześnie, w wieku 12 lat, więc silne, jeszcze dziecięce przeżywanie świata wokół mnie i dotykających mnie zdarzeń złączyło się w moim przypadku z pierwszymi próbami artystycznego uchwycenia i zatrzymania tych silnych wzruszeń i doznań. Do tej pory doskonale pamiętam moje wczesne włóczęgi po wiejskiej okolicy gospodarstwa mojej prababki w poszukiwaniu miejsc i sytuacji, które w niewytłumaczalny sposób mnie zachwycą, będą rodzajem „dotknięcia metafizycznego" czy wręcz epifanii. To było jak radość odcyfrowywania wielkich tajemnic zakodowanych w nieznanym języku, przeżywanie niecodziennych doznań, które domagały się jakiegoś osobistego, artystycznego zapisu, który dałby mi szansę podzielić się tą estetyczną i metafizyczną radością z innymi. Świetnym probierzem było to, czy samo obcowanie z miejscem lub zdarzeniem wywoływało we mnie tzw „gęsią skórkę" i czy także ich przetworzenia w postać obiektu artystycznego wzbudzały podobny stan.

Mając poczcie, że moje własne próby artystyczne bezustannie krążą wokół objawień i miejsc świata mego dzieciństwa, tych realnych, zmitologizowanych lub rozpoznanych w innych projekcjach i miejscach, tym bardziej cieszą mnie i inspirują dzieła innych autorów, którzy także eksplorują świat dziecięcych, najczęściej własnych fascynacji. Z natury rzeczy do tego najlepszym medium jest literatura i poezja. Stąd też taką przyjemność zrobiła mi lektura wierszy poety Michaela Burnsa, z tomiku, dla którego niedawno opracowywałem okładkę. Mimo, że dzieciństwo i młodość jego i moja upłynęły po dwóch stronach dzielącej ówczesny świat „żelaznej kurtyny", w innych krajach, warunkach politycznych i ekonomicznych, z wielkim wzruszeniem odkryłem w jego wierszach ten sam żar, siłę i tajemnicę pierwszych dziecięcych czy młodzieńczych objawień, przefiltrowaną dyskretnie przez perspektywę dojrzałego wieku. To ten sam rodzaj radości jaką dawała mi lektura tomów nieśmiertelnej powieści Marcela Prusta „W Poszukiwaniu Straconego Czasu" czy pow-

Landscape with the Windmill by Jacek Frączak

ieści polskiego pisarza Wiesława Myśliwskiego pt. „Widnokrąg". Myślę, że stałe poszukiwanie w sobie zdolności zdziwienia i zachwytu, ale też i sposobu przeżywania cierpienia jakie dane są dzieciństwu to rodzaj autentycznego napędu, który wg definicji Franka Stelli, może najlepiej przetworzyć się w fakt estetyczny, przywracający sztuce jej sens i wagę.

Missouri Waltz by Jacek Frączak

Aleksander Lewin

Gdy nadchodził kres...

*Ostatnie lata życia
Janusza Korczaka*

ISBN 83-02-06375-4

9 788302 063756

96 r. — Cena zł 10,00
100 000

Book Cover by Jacek Frączak

Art and the Child

In the first chapter of his famous and provocative book, *The End of Art* (Cambridge, 2004), the author, critic, and art historian Donald Kuspit recounts the opinion of Frank Stella—the "Old Master of Modern Art"—regarding the 2001 MoMa exhibition, "Modern Starts," curated by John Elderfield. His radically critical if not demolishing view of the exhibition also declared Mr. Stella's diagnosis of the shallow, banal role that contemporary art has assumed in society. As Mr. Stella noted, contemporary art is reduced to a vehicle of mass entertainment or, somewhat less banal, to an object of financial speculation and investment. As both Donald Kuspit and Frank Stella emphasize, modern art has eliminated aesthetic experience from its inventory of applied vital elements. Aesthetic experience—that absolutely unique, undemocratic state of mind and soul—offers a sort of temporary "revelation," a "metaphysical touch" and relief from the banality of daily life and the sufferings that accompany it. That unique spiritual/intellectual state of momentary, highly intense experiencing of the world (and of one's self in the center of it) both Kuspit and Stella compare to childhood experience generally, childhood being the most pristine, creative, and sensitive time of experiencing one's unique existence.

Many of my own artworks either directly recall images of children or attempt to create visual compositions filled with an excitement for the world—with a revelation I still remember from my childhood. These may be some special places portrayed directly, but most commonly they are recreated and transformed to accord with the "magic" they once afforded me. I have practiced visual art since I was twelve years old, so fresh and strong experiencing of the world around me (and of the important events that were part of my life)

Portret of Zuzanna by Jacek Frączak

was combined with my first attempts at grabbing, recording, and defining my emotions and experiences in artistic form. Even now, I remember so well my teenaged wanderings in the countryside of my Grandmother's farm in search of places that could offer me some mysterious, ultimate delight, that could be like an epiphany or "metaphysical touch," though without any explicit cause. It was like the joy of being able to decipher some great secret written in an unknown language. It was like experiencing totally fresh and unique perspectives, which one then feels an urge to share with others in very personal, emotional, and artistic ways. And the best test of it was when a place or event that affected me with "goose bumps" did the same with others, who could see the aesthetic transformation of these same places and/or events into art.

The more I explore the revelations and places of the world of my own childhood—those real ones, those mythologized, and those others recognized/imagined in different places or projections—the more delighted I am by the masterpieces of those who themselves take artistic advantage of the worlds of their childhood. Poetry and the novel by definition are among the best media for doing that, which is why I was so excited to read *"Night of the Grizzly"* (Moon City, 2011), a posthumous collection of poems by Michael Burns for which I recently designed the book cover. Despite the fact that our childhood and youth belonged to opposite sides of the "Iron Courtain," being in different countries and in different political and economic systems, to my greatest joy and surprise I discovered so much that we had in common. In his poems I found the same tension, strength, passion, and heat of a child's and teenager's revelations, though discreetly filtered through the wisdom and self-consciousness of maturity. This was the same kind of aesthetic excitement and emotional revelation that I remember from reading Marcel Proust's immortal *In Search of Lost Time* and the Polish Wiesław Myśliwski's novel, *Widnokrąg* ("The Horizon"). I believe that one's (rather, my own?) never-ending search and reaching-out for that special sensitivity, for that openness and curiosity, and also for that direct experience of suffering that children can achieve may fuel—as Frank Stella suggests—the true aesthetic experience, thus regaining for the visual arts their wonted sense and importance.

Great Wandering by Jacek Frączak

Burton Raffel

A Jewish Child, Hungary, 1943

Felix Steinberg, six years old,
stands near the end of a line, facing
the Danube, holding his father's hand,
understanding nothing. The line
keeps moving toward the river, as people
up on front keep falling down.
He cannot ask
his father, who stands silent,
like all the others. And then he sees
soldiers, rifles raised, shooting at
those in the very front, and soldiers
throwing bags of garbage into
the river. The bags are people turned
to garbage. The line moves forward,
and still he does not understand.

And then the shooting stops, and those
who are not dead are free to go home.
Holding his father's hand, Felix
walks slowly home, afraid
of being turned to garbage, rotting deep
in the river, comprehending nothing
but fear, which now he knows
is all he as a Jew has any need to know.

Caleb True

Sugar in Wartime

My mother and I watch a column of fresh soldiers march down Nevskii Prospect. They avert their eyes, refuse to look at us. We are apparitions of death to these men. The Germans are only four kilometers away. To the north, the Finns. These men are marching to the German front.

I remember standing and watching these men when I was fourteen and my mother took me to this same street, to a small French café. Now the Prospect was a canyon of jagged edges and broken glass. With the first blizzard, the street was turned into a series of ice caves. Those bombed out of their apartments on the upper stories built fires in the ruins of entranceways. One of those entranceways had been the French café, and in there, five years ago, my mother and I had sat in our finest dresses tasting desserts. It was a special outing without my father, and my mother shocked me by pointing out men in the café and asking how I found them. No one will judge you, she said. You're becoming a woman now.

My mother's voice was different then. Her face was plump with love and happiness and food. She had a good job and my brother wasn't in the army yet. I was about to enroll in school because, as my mother proudly said, Comrade Stalin knows the importance of educating women and men alike. In that café, my mother leaned in close. You're a beautiful girl, she said, and she was right. I had curves at fourteen. I had slender calves. I had dark, bright eyes. My mother said that I had her legs, but I could see she had the stilts of a grand piano. My mother must have been pretty when she was younger. The waitress brought us a small dish. I had never seen crème brûlée before. It looked like filthy brown ice. What is it, I asked my mother. Try some, she said. It's a French decadence. And she

161

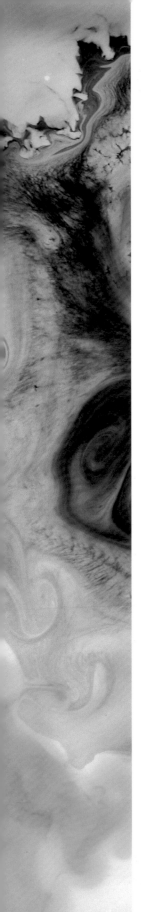

took a spoon and shattered the surface. There was cream inside. I tried some, and the ice was so sweet. It's not cold, I said. It's sugar, said my mother, burned into a sheet by fire.

The soldiers are long gone, the last of them having turned the corner. A wind blows up, and the crowd of shambling onlookers all turn their backs to the gust. I shiver, and my mother jerks her head, time to go home. I follow my mother's vagabond form through snowy streets. She has lost most of her middle over the past few months. Since the time we were on the Prospect sharing crème brûlée, five years ago, my mother has lost all her contentedness, all her glow and optimism, and her body has followed suit. It was strangely sagging now, having gained so much weight in a normal womanly way, over two decades, and having lost again it so quickly, and at an age when skin does not stretch anymore.

Arriving back at our home, my mother immediately slices my bread ration. Things looking up, she says. She hands over the piece, four centimeters thick. This is too much, I say. She ignores me, goes into the living room. I am going on watch, she says. See you in the morning. I follow my mother to the back door, where a makeshift series of scaffolds lead to the roof of our building. My mother has two buckets of sand with her. If an incendiary bomb were to come down on our building, my mother would put it out with the sand. She lifts one bucket, placing it in front of her, one level up on the scaffolding, then lifts the other, then lifts herself, one foot at a time, panting. She turns to me. Go and rest.

The Germans bombed the food warehouses first. In the earliest days of September, when Kiev had been destroyed, and Lvov, and Minsk, the Germans sent in their bombers and set the city on fire. They didn't bother the troop transports, the trains of firewood, or the gun emplacements set up along the mouth of the Neva. They bombed the food and the neighborhoods. They put shells in the courtyard of the winter palace, destroying the fountain and killing all the gardeners. My father worked in the factory sector, and he said when the bombs hit one warehouse, you could smell baking bread in the streets for a few moments, until the smell

162

turned to burnt bread, to carbon and the sickly sweet smell of something ruined. There was a legend that the sugar processing plant had been hit by an incendiary bomb, flash-liquefying eleven tons of sugar within a few seconds before hardening it into carbon slag. All the supply routes in the city were cut off by November, and what food was left was locked up in bank vaults to be rationed day by day.

I was worried, sitting in the café with my mother five years ago, that the desserts we ate would make me fat. No good socialist boy will marry a fat girl, I said. Eat, eat, said my mother, you are fourteen. If you don't fatten up at least in some places, no good socialist boy will want you any-how. She lowered her voice, and said to me something about how even the fat girls have men waiting to love them, and the world can be a very cold place sometimes.

I sit in the living room, bundled in a blanket, savoring the slice of bread that was dinner and lunch and breakfast. I have my knees pulled up to my chest. My left arm holds my legs close. The blanket covers me; just my right arm pokes out, holds the bread slice. I nibble at it, taking mouse bites. I stare out the window. On the iced-over walls of the build-ing across the street, I see the reflection of rooftops. I see figures moving around up there, and one of them is my mother. Two nights ago it was forty degrees below zero, and she kept watch all night. She says the Ger-mans do not bomb when there are people out watching. It is superstition, I know, because truly they want everyone in the city to die, but it is like a pot of water. If it is watched, it seems never to boil. I nibble at my bread, turn the shrinking piece over with my fingers. There are bits in it that I cannot eat: rocks, wood shavings, unidentifiables. I let these bits soak in my mouth for a while, then spit them out. Underneath the blanket, I hook the thumb and forefinger of my left hand around my calf, just below the knee. I can make my fingertips touch. Night comes on slow with barely a change in the color of the sky. It was gray for hours, then a darker slate. Time passes and the sky brightens again. With the rising sun comes shelling from the south.

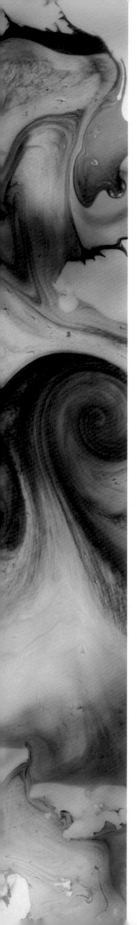

I startle awake, shaking loose a cascade of inedible bread bits. I'm still on the floor, cocooned in my blanket. Outside, the morning sledge-puller passes by. A single soldier follows the sledge-puller. My mother comes in from the kitchen. She draws the shades. Go to the back of the house, she says. She grabs me by my arm and lifts me from my crouch, from the folds of the blanket. I did not resist as she led me to the kitchen and placed me in the pantry, closing the door. Mother did not want me to see the sledge-pullers. She did not want them to see me either. She knew that if they saw me, they would put me to work, make me a sledge-puller. I told my mother at one time that if it was my duty to be a sledge-puller, I would do it, but she just glared. You are not to participate, she said simply.

The sledge-pullers only became a daily thing when the bread rations were cut for the fifth time. My mother was allocated 125 grams. I was allocated 125 grams. It was rumored that my father, still a factory worker, was getting nearly 700 grams, but we had not seen him since November. To conserve energy, all the factory workers stopped returning home to sleep at night, sleeping instead in the factories, beside their work. We had no idea if my father was still alive or not. Every time a sledge-puller came by, I thought about my father and if he was warm enough. The sledges were always full. Many pairs of feet stuck out from beneath a tarp. The sledge puller would stop and knock at intervals along our street, at doors, at window frames, sometimes at a slab of ice acting as barrier between shelter and snowdrift. The sledge-puller was looking for the dead, or for young people like me who could be sledge-pullers. The soldier with the gun was there to help people volunteer. It was rumored that the soldier's gun was unloaded, to save bullets.

I know better than to ask my mother if father is going to come home at any point. I know he cannot, at least until he can be fed enough to make the trip and perform his labors. In the spring, my mother would say. Father will come home in the spring. Until then mother and I spend our days moving slowly, conserving energy, and heat, and hope.

164

Today it is mid-afternoon. My mother and I play chess in the kitchen at the back of the house. We are playing on a burlap sack. We drew the chessboard on the burlap sack with a piece of coal. The original board, a finely carved maple thing, was split for firewood. The kitchen is bare, but there is a loaf of bread in the steel breadbox, and a half-shaker of salt, which we put to our tongues to alleviate hunger pangs. The salt makes my taste buds squirt and my heart race, sends shivers through me, but I try not to do it because I don't want my mother to think I am hungry. The last time she thought that, she went across town to the bombed out warehouses to look for food, risking arrest.

When my mother is asleep or out on watch, I listen to the radio. The radio reminds us that we are heroes for staying alive. All I have done is exactly that. Stay alive, nothing more. Play chess. I at times feel very helpless. My mother won't even let me haul corpses. The radio reminds us to occupy ourselves and live the revolution day-to-day. Keep a diary, keep sane. Resist the fascists. Resist the fires. Share warmth. Conserve food, conserve fuel. Resist death. My mother snorts. She says she has been through worse things. When she was a toddler, the Neva flooded, killing her aunt and uncle. When she was a young woman, like me, she spent a winter in an apartment overlooking Nevskii Prospect during the civil war. All you could do, she said, was steal food, try not to get shot, and make love slowly to stay warm. When I was your age, she said to me, there was no ration, only theft. With Yudenich and the Whites marching on the city, your father and I stole fifteen loaves of bread and a sack of sugar from an abandoned bakery. We snuck the food up to our apartment, and did not leave the bedroom for a month.

Sometimes, if I brush the radio dial with a finger, I can catch, for a moment, the pirate signal from the Germans, crackling with static. They also ask us to resist. In Prussian-accented Russian, they say that Comrade Stalin has left us to starve to death, that no relief will come. Declare the great city of Petersburg an open city, and we will bring you grain, and sugar. Warmth, and fuel. The Germans would only acknowledge the

city's imperial name. If my mother caught me listening to the Germans, I don't know what she would do.

One time in mid-September, when we were caught underground during a raid, I asked my mother if we were going to die. The bombs stomped around above us. Dust came down; the crackling of a nearby fire grew louder. God will protect us, my mother said. When she said that, I looked at the others in the basement. They hadn't noticed, or had otherwise simply understood, given the circumstances. Mother, I hissed, how can you speak of God? How can you deny the utility of life? The words came so quickly. They were words from school, from dialectical materialism, from a German long dead, and my mother's hand shot from her coat and clamped onto my forearm. She didn't say a word, she just glared at me, and, as the bombs shook the eaves and dust sprinkled our hair, I could see through her eyes to a place before the revolution, where people didn't have to trade God for hope, hope for dialectical materialism, the triptych for the Central Executive Committee.

It was the end of another day, and my mother was hauling her sand buckets to the roof for watch. She propped herself up, hand to knee, with each lift gasping for breath. Please, mother, let me help you. I can take watch tonight, I said. I reached to relieve her of one bucket. No, she spat, and shrugged me away, losing her balance. She came down hard on the slats crisscrossing the scaffolding. One bucket overturned, sending sand into the air, falling faster than snow, dusting the ground brown. Idiot, cried my mother, lying there half-dying in front of me, refusing my assistance. Mother, I said, Please. Get back in the house, my mother said. I stood my ground. The rations are improving, I said. I have the energy. I can do night watch. I can pull a sled. Please mother, I said, this is so selfish! My mother got to her feet with great effort, her jaw set. She took a deep breath. I cannot let you, she said.

I left the house, skirting the building so my mother couldn't spot me. I hadn't been out since the troops had marched through town, days ago. I headed in the direction of the factory district, determined to find my fa-

166

ther. He would understand my desire to work. I cut through the center of town. The night was silent; the searchlights were the only thing moving, tracing crosshatches on the low cloud cover. I came out from between buildings to the great square before the Winter Palace. Enormous guns pointing at the sky surrounded the palace like saluting stumps. Dotting the square before the Winter Palace were oval shadows, deep craters in the snow. Approaching the rims of each crater, I noticed familiar pale forms, the starved nude, in stacks. No one had the energy to dig graves anymore. Major craters were repurposed. Without intending to, I scanned the faces for my father as I hurried past.

My mother tried to protect me from all the death at first. She gave up when it was hopeless, too obvious. Every day I more closely resembled those in the craters, those on the sledge. My small breasts had shrunk to deflated pigs' bladders. My collarbone threatened to push through my skin, and after while it hurt to stand for more than a few minutes at one stretch. What I can't see, I told my mother, I can smell. Even the coldest days of winter could not hide the stench when the winds picked up. My mother looked at me pityingly when I told her that. To my mother, I had become this young woman, something that has to do with talking frankly about sex. But she was not yet ready, I think, for me to become an adult, something that has to do with talking frankly about death. Still, she hides me in the pantry every time the sledge-pullers pass by.

I aimed for the last factory I knew of where my father was employed. It was tucked in along the easternmost edge of the factory district, near the food warehouses that had been targeted. If he were still there, he'd just be lying down for the night. I did not notice it at first, but everything was abandoned. The buildings stood, but were shells. Winter winds blew snow in and out of doorways. I circled around to the edge of the district, straddling the canal. I moved in among the buildings, the husks of fac-tories, searching for something. I came finally to a building that looked almost intact. Glass windows on its outside were unshattered, some uncracked even. A poster above the main double doors of the factory cel-

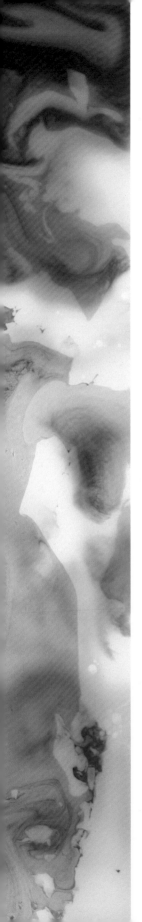

ebrated a steadfast and noticeably plump, integrated workforce. One man had a bread paddle across his shoulder like a rifle. The woman had her fists on her hips and a bonnet on her head. Another man carried a sack. The idea of carrying anything made my arms ache from the shoulders down. I went inside to find not a factory full of sleeping men, nor my father, but an enormous frozen mass. It was the sugar processing plant, and the legend was true. Above me hung a conglomeration of the upper three stories, destroyed, fused into an enormous boulder of charred sugar. Icicles hung from the walls and from the boulder. Sugar explosions had frozen in place, amber blooms in the air. The floor, had it not been frozen solid, would have sucked my shoes off from the stickiness. The floor was a warm brown color like crème brûlée.

I was about to kneel down and lick the floor when I heard the drone of German planes. Silence, in an instant, was replaced by a whole host of sounds. The big guns in front of the Winter Palace went off. A dog somewhere started barking. Men hollered at each other, men who I hadn't seen or heard or seen footprints of, anywhere near the factory district. The threat of death had brought the desolate place to life. The air rumbled, the ground quaked. I could feel the reload recoil of the Winter Palace guns in the soles of my feet. Icicles, and an amber sugar star from high above came tinkling to death on the floor. The enormous boulder of blackened sugar shook ominously, and I moved to the far corner of the factory, out from beneath it. There was a crash and a closer boom, and I was thrown off my feet. There was a flash, I blinked, and found myself facing half the building ablaze. Light flickered, heat radiated. Sirens went off, and there was machine gun fire, it seemed, right outside the building. I tried to get up, but my hands were stuck to the ground. The floor was melting. I pulled my hands out of the slop and licked them. The sugar made my taste buds squirt and my heart race, sending shivers through me. I licked every one of my fingers, then started wading, with difficulty, across the floor towards the wall of fire. I didn't even think of the danger. I was mesmerized by sweetness and heat, like some insect in the mouth

168

of a carnivorous plant, swimming in sugar, stupefied by decadence, twiddling the plant's feelers from the inside out. Another bomb burst to life behind me, another wall of flame went up. I threw off my coat, still wading forward. I reached down as I went, brought up another finger of burnt syrup. There was grit and bits of glass in the syrup, but I spat them out. Then a man burst into the plant. I saw him through the shimmering heat. He started towards me, then shrunk away from flames eating up the entranceway. He beckoned for me to get out of there. I shook my head. Out there was only coldness and sledge-pullers, craters and dry bread. How much bread, I thought for a moment, licking my fingers. How many grams? How much firewood had mother and I spared whenever nights hovered at a tolerable zero? Another explosion brought a wall of glass down on me, sending me to my knees. One knee was bloody. Syrup mixed with blood on the floor, and I swirled it pink and gold, then brought my fingers to my lips again, salty-sweet. I looked towards the door and the man was gone.

I was not rescued by anyone that night at the processing plant. I must have fallen asleep at some point, relaxed by heat, nourished by sugar to the point of ecstasy and headaches. By morning, the fire was out, the heat swallowed up again by the cold, by the snow and ice, by silence. I unstuck myself from the floor and wandered home. When I rounded the corner to our street, I came upon the sledge at rest. The guard with no bullets stood beside the sledge, rifle slung round his shoulder, hands crammed deep in his pockets. He must have seen me coming, or very nearly smelled me. He turned, his eyes widening at the crystallizations all over my coat. He traced the stain from where it dusted the snow at my heels to where it met my hair, and then he finally looked at me. I hugged the coat around myself more tightly, took two steps back. It was all I could do to prevent the guard dropping to his knees right there and sucking my hem, lapping the burnt sugar like a dog, but just then my father came out of our building. I cried out. My cry broke the guard's hypnosis. I ran to my father. I slammed into him, burst into tears. He held me. Father, I said.

I told him that I had searched for him all night. I told him I got caught in the sugar factory during the raid and had to stay there till morning. I told him mother wouldn't let me do anything, she was so weak and yet she wouldn't let me do anything to help. Darling, my father said, and he squeezed me close to his chest where I could hear his heart beating and feel every jutting rib. Darling, you've done everything you possibly can. I looked up at his hard, cracked face. Darling, you're alive.

I found out afterwards that my mother had been giving me her portion of the rations. Her 125 grams. This kept me alive. My mother had consumed little more than tea with glue shavings for weeks, hauling buckets, watching rooftops, ushering me to the back of the house when the sledge-puller came looking for the dead, or the able-bodied to haul the dead. My mother made me think things were getting better before they actually did get better, in January, when Lake Ladoga froze solid and trucks with food could make it into the city. My mother refused to let me work. She refused me any part in the war effort. She wanted me only to pray, if I would, even if the praying had to do with dialectical materialism and not God. She wanted, as I wished, that someday again boys would gaze justifiably at my beauty, and hunger, like a guard with no bullets, for the mere hems of my coat.

Joseph Cover

Execution of Responsibility

The Saturday following opening day of bow season, I was up before dawn and banging on the door to my Uncle Jimmy's two-bedroom stucco farmhouse. I had recently turned thirteen and he had promised to take me on my first deer hunt, which was the only way my mom, Jimmy's sister, was going to let me go. I could still hear my mom's car driving down the lane when Jimmy's girlfriend, Megan, greeted me at the door and ushered me towards the Formica table. The normally stale air in his house was filled with the fragrance of Megan's shampoo.

"You're up?" I asked.

She smiled and patted my hair, "Stayed up all night just to see you, Buddy. I even showered for you."

Though she was easily twenty years my senior, I was captivated by Megan, who had been living with Jimmy for about a month now. I watched her move quietly through the kitchen. Her flannel robe, pulled tight at the waist, accented her figure. Slight cleavage showed through the gap at the top of her robe. Without makeup her skin had a natural auburn tone. Freckles danced lightly across her cheeks, and her eyes were round, brown, and accented with long black lashes. Her smooth legs were connected to her bare feet with perfectly sculpted ankles. At that moment, I had the desire to just reach out and take her hands in mine, draw close, and be engulfed by her essence.

Setting a cup of coffee before me, she asked, "What'll it be, Buddy, Eggos or Quaker Oats?"

"Eggos."

"All righty," she replied, pulling her coarse red hair into a ponytail and tying it with a thick black band she had around her wrist. I watched her

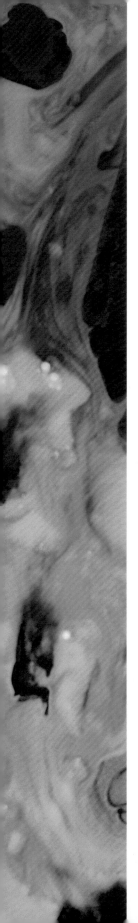

brown checked robe gently sway as she moved across the kitchen to the freezer and to the toaster.

"Where's Jimmy?"

"Passed out. He won't be up for a while, but yesterday he set you up a ladder to that tree stand in the oak on the north side of the barn. Eat these Eggos and get on up there. He said deer pass by there moving from the fields to the woods down by Clear Creek. Where's your gun?"

"My bow's outside. No gun. It's bow season. It's a felony to even carry a gun when bow hunting, much less use one."

She sat the waffles in front of me and smiled. "Well, then, don't be carrying no guns today. Wouldn't want to see my Buddy going to the pen."

I wolfed down the waffles, headed out the door, and glanced back to catch Megan looking over her shoulder in my direction, but her brown eyes seemed distant, as if she were seeing something a thousand miles away. I grabbed my Bear Archery compound bow with a camo tape-covered metal handle and fiberglass limbs imprinted with the words Whitetail Hunter around a drawing of a buck's head and headed across the feedlot towards the barn.

The damp October morning air was refreshed by a slight breeze. Excitement made my step feel light as I dodged cow pies, fresh and dried, on the hard-packed dirt around the barn. The oak stood just far enough from the barn that the widest branches missed touching the wall. Running up the side of the tree was a pale green metal ladder attached to a two-man tree stand about fifteen feet above the ground. There was a length of baling twine dangling from the stand. I gave the twine a tug to be sure it was secure, and I tied it through the top wheel on the bow, and once in the stand, I used the twine to pull the bow to me.

The tree stands I've seen in the Cabela's catalogue have a safety bar to prevent the hunter from falling and a seat to rest in while tethered to the tree with a safety harness, but Jimmy had made this one out of metal grating from a leftover walkway when they moved the Zenith television factory to Mexico. There was no seat, and it was framed and attached to

172

the tree with angle iron. I sat on the edge and dangled my legs over the side. I laid the bow beside me, removed the quiver, and notched an arrow, placing the shaft on the arrow rest so when a deer came along all I would have to do was pick up the bow and draw the string. I was ready.

I had spent the previous summer getting ready. Buying the bow, arrows, points, and targets, including a 3-D buck with replaceable inserts over the kill zone, consumed most of the money I had earned hauling hay. Just learning to hit the targets cost me at least two dozen arrows, yet every morning by sunrise, I was outside practicing until I could consistently nail targets at twenty, thirty, and forty yards. I practiced standing, kneeling, and sitting. By now, I was more than proficient enough to take down a deer.

To the east I noticed what appeared to be car lights coming down the lane, but these were only the first rays of the sun cresting over the horizon and filtering through the trees along the edge of Clear Creek. I watched the fields to the west for any activity. The cold metal of the tree stand was making my ass numb, so I picked up the bow and stood for a while, leaning up against the tree's rough bark. There was a harness tied to the tree and I slipped it on, but I couldn't sit while wearing it, so after what seemed to be an hour of standing, I took it off and sat down again at the edge of the stand.

I sat there and waited. I laid the bow next to me. Then I held it. I laid it down again and stood up. I sat down again. I began to wish I had brought something to read. A portable television would be nice. As I waited, the sun rose higher in the sky. Still no sign of deer. I dozed, jerked myself awake, and slowly drifted off again only to be awakened by the heaviness of my head lolling backward. I finally surrendered, curled into a ball on the platform of the tree stand, and fell asleep.

The soft patter of feet filtered through my ears. Deer! I sprung awake and grabbed my bow. Scrambling to my knees I drew the arrow and spun in the direction of the sound just to see Jimmy standing on the ladder, inches from me. He smiled with a mouth too large for his egg-shaped head. His face had a flattened appearance where a cow had kicked him, shattering his nose. He had waist-length straight black hair, and few people who didn't know him would guess that he was a successful cattleman. Knuckles battered from hard work and fistfights held out a small backpack as Jimmy said, "Whoa, there, Buddy. Don't shoot. I'm friendly."

We sat side by side as he pulled a thermos from his pack and used the lid to pour me a cup of coffee. Taking a collapsible cup from the pocket of his Carhartt overalls, he poured himself one before he said, "You gotta stay awake to shoot a deer."

"Yeah. Fell asleep."

He ran his finger along the edge of the corrugated steel floor of the stand. "This isn't the best place for napping, and even as big as this stand is, you roll the wrong way, you're going down. Ground's going to hurt."

I looked down. "I didn't see any deer."

"I know. The waiting can be long, but when you see one…." Jimmy's voice trailed off as he stared towards the west. He shook his head. "When you shoot one, you forget all about the waiting." He lightly punched me on the left shoulder. "Get one this year, and you can be bragging at Thanksgiving."

When my family gathered for Thanksgiving dinner, sitting around the table passing mashed potatoes and turkey, we talked hunting. Although my dad didn't hunt, all three of my mother's brothers, and their kids, did, and at every get-together, the oldest brother, Bob, would try to talk Jimmy into selling his Belgium Browning over-under twelve-gauge shotgun. "Jimmy, before you go pawning that thing, sell it to me. I'll give you six, maybe even seven hundred for it."

To which Jimmy would hold up three fingers and reply, "You know it's worth three grand. But I'll just be holdin' on to it awhile longer."

Thanksgiving, coming on the heels of gun season, the real talk centered on deer hunting, and the relatives would share their newest, or most favored, adventures. Bob would tell about the time he shot a buck in deer camp. As he told it, he was sitting on an upturned piece of firewood and eating a hot dog when he noticed a twelve-point buck sneaking through the woods. Leaving the hot dog in his mouth, Bob leaned over, picked up his 30-30, aimed just ahead of where the buck was traveling, and when he stepped into the line of fire, Bob dropped him, as they always did, in one fatal shot, at which time he set the rifle down and finished his lunch before going to dress the deer.

I turned as Jimmy pulled a couple of peanut butter sandwiches from his pack. "Megan sent these over. Got a couple apples, too." My heart swelled as I realized how lucky Jimmy was to have a woman like Megan. What I didn't realize was that less than two weeks later she would disappear in the middle of the night taking her clothes, the money in Jimmy's wallet, and his Belgium Browning, and leaving him with a broken heart and hepatitis C.

"Where'd you meet Megan?"

"At Hilltop over on old 66. She showed up with someone else, but after a night of dancing, she left with me."

I knew the place. It was an old two-story house just outside Halltown where a bootlegger ran an unlicensed bar. I'd been in there once with my dad, and I could see myself with Megan, gliding across the dance floor, holding her close, feeling her breasts pressed into me. It was me she went home with that night instead of Jimmy.

We sat quietly drinking our coffee, lost in our thoughts for several minutes. Jimmy finally spoke. "It's just a little after noon. Sunset's about six-thirty so we got a few more hours. You wanting to stay?"

"I'm not leaving 'til I get my deer."

Jimmy winked. "That's the spirit."

I stood and scanned the tree line from the creek to the field, looking for any sign of action. "Jimmy, where's your bow?"

"Didn't bring it. Today's 'bout you getting a deer. Got your tags? Right?"

I pulled them out of my hip pocket. "Just like you told me."

"Good deal, Buddy."

With the exception of stirring once to go pee off the back of the tree

175

stand, and missing as I tried to shoot the stream onto the side of the barn, the rest of the afternoon passed in long periods of silence punctuated with brief discussions about the best way to skin a squirrel or fry frog legs or how Jimmy would help me fix up Grandad's old pickup. Mostly it was silent waiting. Sitting. Looking. Standing. Snapping to attention at every twig-snap, leaf-rustle, or footfall, only to find a squirrel running through the woods. Then more waiting. Looking, listening.

The sun had just begun to spray its final rays through the treetops as it lowered itself behind the ridgeline at the far edge of the hay field when I saw her. My chest tightened. The doe's step was gentle as her auburn body emerged from the woods and entered the trail that ran along the barn and just below the tree stand. Her path was taking her under us, making a clean shot difficult. Trembling hands held my bow as I carefully drew the string, raised the bow, and considered how best to take the shot. I wanted to ask Jimmy, but I didn't dare speak for fear of spooking her.

She stopped about twenty-five yards from the stand. Her head went up and she began to sniff the air. Her head turned from the right to the left and she seemed to inhale deeply. Her tail twitched up then she lowered it. A wave of remorse swept over me when I realized that, even through the barnyard smells of cattle dung and hay, she had probably scented my urine from earlier. Remorse gave way to hyperventilation as she turned in the trail and stopped. She was standing as still and lifeless as my 3-D target. I could visualize the lines of the replaceable insert around her lungs. I peered through the peep sight and lined her up halfway between the twenty- and thirty-yard pins.

I don't remember releasing the string, only hearing the arrow whisper through the air as my hand rested peacefully against my cheek. Instead of falling over dead, she jumped and ran towards the nearest brush.

Lowering the bow, I turned to Jimmy who was standing, arms folded, and staring at the spot where the doe had stood. Without as much as a twitch he whispered, "You got her, Buddy. You got her."

176

"I missed."

"No. I don't think you did. Let's check it out."

I stepped too quickly, bumped into Jimmy, and dropped my bow to the ground causing the string to pop out of the cable. I looked at Jimmy who only shrugged his shoulders and said, "Can't worry with that now; we don't have a press out here. Let's go find her."

Once on the ground we went to where she had stood. Jimmy squatted low and began searching the area. "Don't see no blood. Course that don't mean much." He pulled a small plastic bottle from his pack and began spraying a mist on the ground. "Peroxide," he explained. "Foams when it hits blood." There was a slight amount of foam. Five, six drops at the most. "I knew you hit her. Let's go."

My heart soared as my feet took flight behind Jimmy. We had just landed in the tree line when he stopped and raised his hand. There she was, maybe twenty yards away. She stood stiff, head high, breathing deeply. Jimmy raised his hand as if to say stop. "She's in shock. Come on." We approached her slowly. She stood her ground.

We came along side her. I'd been around dead deer, and of course my life-size 3-D target, but somehow, standing there she seemed larger than I thought she would be. The evening air was filled with the pungent odor of decaying leaves and dirt, and I heard a squirrel scampering through the leaves. The doe didn't move, but I heard the sound of water hitting the ground as she urinated inches from me. Jimmy's eyebrows arched as he shook his head. We had been standing beside her for a minute, watching her twitch and tremble, when Jimmy reached inside his pack and drew out a Smith & Wesson Snubnose 357. He moved closer to her. I reached out and touched his arm. "It's a felony during bow season."

"She's suffering," Jimmy said. "Might be hours before she drops."

I took a deep breath, held it, and placed my hand on the pistol. I exhaled. "It's my deer. She's my responsibility." I knew what I needed to do. Jimmy wouldn't tolerate letting an animal suffer this way. And I wouldn't either.

He released the pistol, and my hand dropped from its unexpected weight. The grip, smaller in my hand than I would have thought, felt smooth and slick in spite of the checkering.

The doe turned her head and looked at me with round brown eyes. Her long black lashes blinked once, and I heard Megan say, "Wouldn't want to see my Buddy going to the pen."

Under my breath I said, "Even if I go to prison, I'm doing what's right."

A hand rested on my shoulder, and Jimmy whispered in my ear, "I can do it, Buddy. It'll be all right."

But it wouldn't be all right. Whichever way it went, it wouldn't be all right. This wasn't the way it was supposed to go down. I'd watched deer hunting videos, and sometimes the deer drops right away, others the hunter might have to follow a blood trail for fifty or sixty yards, but they always find the deer dead. Last year on opening day, Jimmy took his bow up to the barn loft, saw a buck crossing the field, and dropped him in his tracks at forty-five yards. Never had I heard of anyone shooting a doe execution-style.

The doe's breath came in short shallow gasps. Mine came in long deep draws. My knees were putty as I stepped closer. My arms shook as I raised the pistol.

Jimmy reached for the gun, but I shook him away. I gripped the snub-nose with both hands and placed the barrel where her skull met her spine. Her left eye rolled in my direction and my eyes closed as I squeezed the trigger. I saw myself handcuffed, a deputy's hand on my head, guiding me into the squad car, Megan's arm around the shoulders of my crying mother, assuring her that I was a martyr. The explosion jerked my eyes open. The doe was on the ground. Round brown eyes, staring, not seeing.

I lowered the gun. I looked for blood, brains, and bone bits on my shirt, my pants, my hands. Nothing. I was clean.

While Jimmy field-dressed the deer, I ran back to the house and asked Megan to bring the hay truck around the feedlot and as close as possible to the downed doe.

"Buddy, I heard a shot."

"Yea. She was wounded; my bow broke."

"You going to be in trouble?"

"Not if we don't tell anybody."

As the truck pulled to a halt yards from Jimmy and the doe, Megan said, "Then we won't tell anyone."

And that was when it hit me. I wouldn't be sharing this episode with the family this Thanksgiving or with anyone ever. This was before hunters called in their kill by cell phones. To check the deer, we were going to have to take her to the check-in station in Walnut Grove, and I, along with Jimmy, really would go to jail. The world would label us as poachers. Being a kid, I would get out of it with probation, but Jimmy, being thirty-one, would go to prison.

We loaded the doe onto the truck and went back to Jimmy's house. Nobody said a word. Megan gave me a ride home in her Jeep. Instead of being excited to be alone with her, I just looked out the window wishing the night was over. I left the bow where I dropped it. I suppose Jimmy did something with it. I never asked. I never went bow hunting again, and although I went gun hunting with the family a few times as a teenager, I never shot another deer, even when I saw one in season. And to this day, if anyone asks, I tell them that I have never killed a deer.

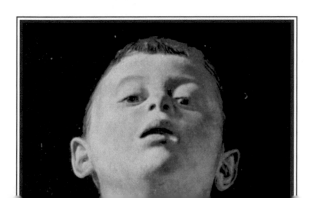

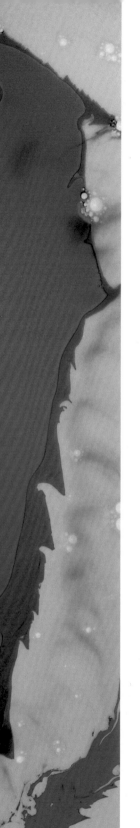

D. Gilson

Macy's Loses Their Art

Mother said *Put it down*
& I tried but the shelf
was up high
      & the snow globe
hit the marble floor with a thud
         with a crackle
and shattered there
          two figures
from the inside broke loose
      I had freed them
but how could they survive
      their ice skates no longer
on that crystal pond
      one missing her left arm
& I swear she was crying
like Mother who grabbed me
with a look & said come
so we ran & ran
      silver bells ran
into the busy sidewalk
city sidewalk—
      who can afford
         to drop everything
just to watch the snow
      fall and gather?

Shiloh Peters

Rewrite of the Old Unrequited Love Sonnet

Dear Journal: Yesterday in science class
my not-named crush was assigned to my group
to dissect that sheep's eye, and when he passed
me the scalpel he said, "You know that soup
in the second Indiana Jones? This
makes me think of that." He spoke to me! Score!!
Dear Journal: I *so* can't concentrate. Miss
Sparks caught him eyeballing Rachel! No, more
like drooling on her. What can he see in
that snotty girl? My life—done. Finito.
Journal, they kissed! I saw it. He's taken,
but he *sooo* has to dump her! God, you know,
nothing feels quite like bird crap from above
like this unrequited junior high love.

Shiloh Peters

Public Works Project №1: Some Words on the Methodology of Ethical Eating

Recently I experienced the irrepressible need to relieve my feelings on a certain subject of much ethical importance: the proper method of eating animal-shaped foods, including, but not limited to, animal crackers, chocolate Easter bunnies, gummy worms and bears, Swedish fish, etc. My social concern about this topic stems from my childhood, during which time I was chastised mercilessly by my female peers and some adults for my head-first biting technique when eating said foods. Being unable to fully articulate an argument for my defense at the time (possibly because my mouth was full), I mutely submitted to being called cruel and, henceforth, blindly followed the lead of others in chewing off the hindquarters of the food product in question, saving the head for last. Eventually my own qualms of conscience forced me to stop eating animal-shaped treats altogether, since my original method was generally considered wrong, and the proscribed method *felt* wrong.

This was a difficult and rather sugarless time for me, as you can well imagine. But the days of my inarticulate youth are now long past; I can indeed explain my own moral stances now. Moreover, I have reached a position of animistic enlightenment that has facilitated a Renaissance of goody consumption in my life. As such, I now consider it my social duty to instruct the unfeeling majority in the ways of true humanity and civilized dining for the good of, and to promote justice for, both the animal-shaped food and the individual in the minority who unpopularly eats it quite properly.

Picture for a moment, if you will, a hunting lion as she makes the final leap towards the terrified, running gazelle. In the work of an instant the delicate gazelle is pinned down, prostrate, and at the mercy of the lion, under whose great paws the pitiable creature will receive neither mercy nor pity. Blind with panic and pain, it continues to cry out and writhe as the lion rips away large chunks of flesh from the *still-conscious* creature. Slowly shock sets in and only the eyes of the gazelle move as they watch the lion leisurely strip bare the bones and lap up the very life-blood of a body that once cavorted on the savannah. When death finally comes for the poor, evolutionarily doomed animal, the relief of oblivion is, understandably, a blessing.

Now, instead of a heartless lion holding a gazelle, picture a child holding a gazelle-shaped cracker in its sticky fingers, poised and ready to take the bite that will lead to destruction. Ladies and gentlemen (if you be such), I leave it to your judgment. Which is the truly cruel child? The one who bites the head off first, ensuring a quick and relatively painless "death," or the one who starts with the back end, prolonging the tortuous pain of the eaten?

To end the clearly appalling aforementioned injustices, I would like to propose the following: a fine in the amount of five cents per bite taken before eating the head of any animal-shaped food shall be extracted from all offending children. Proceeds will be paid directly to me, a portion of which will be allocated for the printing and placement of fliers bearing the image of a headless gummy bear under the motto "Euthanize First— Savor Later: It's the Humane Thing to Do." All remaining proceeds will, of course, be put towards my rent. I thank you for your kind consideration and help in this matter.

Katlyn Minard

Leap

I have a crush on a Bible-beater.

I don't know how it happened.

She's worn the same gold cross around her neck every day for nine years. I know, because we've had classes together ever since elementary school. Back then she was short and scrawny, so the charm dangled down to the middle of her stomach. Now that she's all grown up, it falls right between her breasts. That means every time I stare at them, I have no choice but to stare at the cross as well. I am constantly wondering which trump card is bigger.

Everything about her is ungodly perfect. She's skinny, but not creepy-skinny—not *supermodel*-skinny. Just healthy. Her hair is long and straight and bright blond, kind of like a Barbie's hair, but a lot less fake. She's a model student, a model citizen, and—I'm assuming—a model Christian.

Her name is Alex Lovett. My name is Max McPherson. And she might go out of her way to learn more than my name, if I weren't an out-of-the-closet atheist.

Twelve hundred people in this school. Four hundred juniors, over half of them girls. A *sea* of girls at my disposal, and I've ended up obsessing over a girl who's obsessed with Jesus. Day after day I find myself bemoaning the idea that I have lost out to a fictional character, and today is no exception. Today, in the hazy passing period between history and American lit, I've got it bad.

"God forgive me," I mumble into my locker. "I know not what I do."

I peer over the rim of my glasses to see Alex Lovett opening her locker, which is twenty lockers down from mine. On the inside door of her locker is a picture, a little calendar, a plastic-rimmed mirror she never uses, and a crumpled piece of paper. The picture is of a smiling little blond kid, probably someone in her undoubtedly huge Christian family. I don't know what's up with the piece of paper—it's probably a psalm, or a Bible saying or something. I don't really want to find out, because I like pretending it's a Hunter S. Thompson quote. Or a Karl Marx quote. Something hot like that.

I don't have anything in my locker except for my books. Maybe I would decorate the door, if she could see it from where she stood.

I shove my books into my locker and watch her do the same. She usually takes her time between third and fourth periods, so I usually do, too. The bell won't ring for about three more minutes, giving me plenty of time to mull over my situation and be an über-creeper all at the same time. And the thing is, I'm not an obsessive person. That's why I don't know what the hell is wrong with me. I've been dwelling on it for weeks now and I still can't figure it out. I lie in bed at night, thinking about why I think about her. I think about her. I think about her hair. I think about her ass. I think about her face. Her lips. Her tongue. Her mouth making an O. And that's as far as I get before the fantasy.

"Max!" She slams the door and whirls around, soaked to the skin from the pouring rain.

"I'm through with this," she says, scrambling toward me. "The church, the Bible, my entire life! I'm through with it!" I set down On the Road *and take her by the shoulders.*

"It's all right, it's fine," I tell her. "You don't have to follow their rules anymore. You're free." I reach behind her head and grab her cross necklace, rip it clean off her neck. She gasps.

"You're so strong," she says. "I want to be like you: so brave, so liberal, so fearlessly skeptical!" She touches my cheek. It's a gesture of worship.

"You can be whatever you want," I say, and I take her face in my hands.

She stares at me longingly, trembling, and says, "Teach me."

I kiss her. She kisses me back. She lets me rip off her shirt (which is really hard to do, because it's wet and heavier than normal), lets me grab her all over her flawless, rain-raw body, and she throws her head back and moans, "Oh, God …."

"McPherson!"

I blink. Then again. It takes a minute for me to get back in touch with reality. When I do, it's a rude awakening. I turn around reluctantly to face the last person I want to see right now. "Hi, Bernie."

Bernie is the president of the Flying Spaghetti Monster chapter at our school, and living proof that obnoxious things come in small packages. I once interviewed her for an opinion piece about religion for the *Eagle*, our school newspaper, and she took that as an indication of my support for FSM. So now she keeps me abreast of all their stupid events, hoping that I'll write some hero piece the next time they hold a rally in the courtyard. There are two things Bernie doesn't know, though: 1) Nobody reads the *Eagle*; and 2) I don't give a flying fuck in space about her brigade of loud-mouthed Christian-haters.

"Heads up, McPherson—we've got trouble. Even the theater department is against us now." Like all Pastafarians, Bernie is incapable of making small talk.

"Exactly how do you mean?" I say, checking my watch.

Bernie's bespectacled eyes get huge. "You haven't heard?" she says. "The theater department is going ahead with their production of *Godspell*, despite the tireless efforts of my people to convince them otherwise. The curtain goes up a week from Friday, McPherson. Do you know what this means?"

I couldn't care less. "That we still don't have enough money to do *Little Shop of Horrors?*" I suggest.

"That our *public school* has approved a play containing *blatant religious bias*, even against the wishes of its students—and that, my friend, is a violation of the separation of church and state."

186

I roll my eyes. "There's nothing you can do about it, Bernie, the play's already happening—and nobody's forcing you to go see it. If you're so pissed about it, why don't you just—"

The sound of a metal door slamming twenty lockers down stops me. My head snaps to the left and I see Alex Lovett sling her backpack over her shoulder. This is really odd, totally irregular. She's deviating from her fourth-period route. She's not going into the science lab. She's walking in my direction.

And here I am, shooting the shit with the female president of FSM. Oh, Jesus Christ, no.

Survival instincts. Cunning. "Bernie, go straight to the theater department if you're upset. I think Ms. LeRoche has a free period right now. Go. Now."

"You're right," she says. "LeRoche likes me. Some of my people are running tech for her. Good thinking, McPherson—I'll update you about the goings-on later. *R'amen!*"

"Whatever," I mutter, and she's gone. Alex Lovett is making her way down the hall, getting closer to me with every step. What is she doing? Her class is the other way. The bell has already rung. Everyone is in class by now—we're the last two people in the hall. Which means ... oh my God, she's coming for me. She's coming to talk to *me*. She's even *looking* at me. I have no idea why this is happening, but I don't have time to figure it out.

I straighten my glasses, tuck in my pockets. She's really close now. I know that because I'm still staring. Oh my *God*, I'm still staring. Look away, jackass! You should be acting casual, you should be rifling through your locker like you don't care, looking like a badass, not continuing to stare at her as she gets closer and closer and—

"Why are you here?"

It's out before I can stop it.

She cocks her head and looks at me like I'm crazy, which isn't far from the truth at this point.

"What?" she says.

I can't think of anything new to say. "Why …." Think, think, think. "Why are you here?" Fail.

She looks around quizzically, possibly for an escape route. "You mean, like … on the Earth?" she says, smiling.

I manage a weak, nervous laugh. "No," I say, "in this hallway. I mean, 'cause, don't you, um, have Ms. Laird's class this hour?"

"Oh," she says. "Yeah, I do. But I get to skip it today, you know, to do my NHS community service hours? I'm going to help paint the set for my church's Easter play this year."

"Well, that's cool," I say. "Have fun re-creating the resurrection, I guess."

"Always do," she jokes. Her gold cross winks at me under the fluorescent lights. "See you later, Max."

She said my name. I have this sudden, intense feeling inside my chest like a match has been struck, and I can't think to do anything but go with it. Which is why I'm still standing here watching her walk up the steps, until….

"Dyouwannagooutsometime?"

She stops midstep, leans over the railing and calls, "What did you say?"

I feel my entire neck get hot, then my ears, then my face. I could run. I could bolt down the hall, feigning concern about my tardiness, and pretend to forget this encounter completely if she asks about it later. Pretend the whole thing never happened.

"I said … do you want to go out sometime. With me."

She stares at me. For just a moment she's concentrating on just me, and it feels like everything has stopped.

"OK."

I blink. Then again. "Really?"

"Sure," she says brightly, and her pale pink lips stretch into a smile. "Why not? How about … are you busy Friday night?"

"Nope," I decide. "Friday night it is, then!"

"Great," she says. "Uh, can we sort out the details later? I have to …." She looks up the stairs.

188

"Sure," I say. "Yeah. Have fun with your, uh, church thing."

She grins at me, then bounds up the stairs two at a time until she's out of sight.

I have a date with Alex Lovett. I am alone in the junior hallway, ten minutes late to American lit, wondering what the hell just happened.

∗ ∗ ∗

"Turn right into Burbank Plaza. Destination is on the left."

Bridget is my GPS tracking instructor. I got a GPS because it freaks me out to be lost, so much so that I even programmed the automated voice to be British, because for some reason the accent soothes me. Bridget's cool voice and foolproof directions usually make me feel safe. Tonight, however, as I pull into the Olive Garden parking lot with Alex Lovett riding shotgun, I could not be more petrified.

"Wow," she says as I park the car. "Really?"

It's a high-rent place for a first date, and she knows it. "Yep," I say, feigning nonchalance. "Because that's how we roll."

"Is it really?" she says playfully.

Sure it is. That, *and* I'm trying desperately to atone for what happened in civics yesterday.

Civics is the only class Alex and I have together this year. Yesterday, our class had a debate: are we in favor of a woman's right to an abortion, or opposed? Mr. Mackey made us travel to opposite sides of the room based on whether we were pro-life or pro-choice, and then we had to construct an argument in favor of our stance. I sat there with the other pro-choice people, trying not to look at Alex, who was sitting on the pro-life side with three other Jesus freaks, conjuring arguments from beliefs I can't even begin to relate to. I mean, how can a woman support the legal regulation of her own body? The whole abortion thing just makes me want to scream. But I didn't. I just kept my head down and my mouth shut, determined not to say anything that would offend Alex and

189

make our date awkward later on. And that worked for a while … until Mr. Mackey selected me to be the spokesperson for our group, based on my enthusiasm for debates in the past. I tried to get out of it, I tried to say that I really didn't have much of an opinion on the subject, but then Bernie's irrepressible voice came from behind me: "Man up, McPherson! Tell 'em the truth—you're a baby-killer and you're proud!"

I wanted to die.

But that was yesterday. That was then, this is now. And right now, I have a gorgeous chick in my car. I have a reservation for two. I have money to burn. I have infinite charm and undeniable charisma. At least, that's what I'm telling myself.

We make our way inside and over to the hostess, who finds my reservation and leads us to a booth almost immediately. Alex looks impressed as she eases into the seat across from me, and I can't help feeling slightly badass. Five points for a killer entrance.

Our bubbly brunette waitress appears to take our drink orders. I let Alex go first. "May I please have … a Shirley Temple?" She asks the waitress, but looks at me. I nod to let her know it's OK. She smiles big at me, then reiterates, "A Shirley Temple, please."

McPherson's batting a thousand so far. Now for the big finish. The waitress scribbles down Alex's order and asks me what I'd like.

I lean back against the booth, give a modest shrug of the shoulders and say, "Just water, please." Then I flash my irresistible nice-guy smile.

Ten points for a flawlessly executed display of coolness. I rule.

Alex looks great tonight. Her white-blond hair is straighter and slinkier than usual. It shines softly under the stained-glass ceiling lamps. Her face glows at me from across the table, and she smiles contentedly. It suddenly hits me that *I* put that smile there, and I feel this sweet kind of warmth flutter around inside me, like when an adult brags about something you've accomplished. It's bliss; I could sit here forever.

All of a sudden it feels like I *have* been sitting here forever. I've just realized that since the waitress left, neither of us has said anything.

"So," I attempt, but nothing comes. I look down into my lap to hide the red in my face.

"So how's your Friday been?" she says.

"Oh," I say, picking my head up. "Pretty good, pretty good. Really good."

"Really good?"

"Yeah, really good," I confirm. "I got to interview Ms. LeRoche about the spring musical, and Bernie came by to commentate, and LeRoche kicked her out." The memory of Bernie's face turning purple with rage makes me smirk. "It was pretty sweet."

Alex tucks her chin to her chest and giggles. "That's not very nice to say about your colleague," she teases.

"Yeah, well," I say. "Bernie's OK. Not that I hang out with her or know her very well at all, really. But she's OK. She's just not the most polite person in the world."

"I know," Alex says, tossing some hair behind her shoulder. "She doesn't strike me as having the best … moral character."

I put down the napkin ring I've been fiddling with.

"Yeah," I say, "I know what you mean."

Actually, I don't know exactly what she means by that. But I'm just gonna go with it.

"I mean, is it really possible for one person to be that rude?" she says with a laugh. "Does she really not understand how offensive all her stupid rants are? It's almost funny."

"Yeah, it is kind of funny." I'm chivalrous, and I'm going with it.

"I just try to tune her out," she says with a shrug. "I learned a long time ago that when people like her get loud, there's really nothing you can do but humor them."

"People like her?" I say, adjusting my glasses.

"Well," she says, "you know.…"

I nod. "Yeah, sure, I know. You're right." Suddenly I'm wondering what the hell is taking our waitress so long.

"I mean, just because *she* prefers to ignore any semblance of a moral code doesn't mean the rest of us want to hear about it."

I adjust my shirt collar. Just go with it.

"It's like, hello, I'm sorry you're so unsatisfied with your own lack of belief that you have to go out of your way to make fun of mine, but really, do you have nothing better to do?"

Go with it. Go with it. Go with it.

She blinks at me. "You OK?"

"Uh, yeah," I lie, wiping the sweat off my forehead. "It's just … hot under these lights."

Alex glances up at the low-watt, stained-glass ceiling lamp and smiles. Looks like she's just gonna go with it, too.

"Oh gosh, look at me," she says, tucking some hair behind her ear. "Sorry, I normally don't ramble like this all the time. It's just a pet peeve of mine."

"No, I get it," I say. "But hey, you shouldn't let Bernie get to you like that. She's a pain, yeah, but she's just speaking her mind. She's harmless, you know?"

"Oh," Alex says, clearing her throat. "Sure. You're right."

She opens up her menu, and all I can do is stare as I realize what's happening. This isn't a real conversation anymore. Alex is humoring me. And as shitty as it feels, I'm not sure how mad I'm really allowed to be, considering that *I've* been humoring *her* this whole time. I rub the bridge of my nose. God help us.

Our waitress finally appears with our drinks. She sets down Alex's Shirley Temple and pours me a much-needed glass of water. "Sorry about the wait. We're understaffed tonight," she explains. She taps my menu and says, "Have you settled on something?"

"No," I say. "We haven't."

She agrees to give us a few more minutes to decide on our dinner, which, I now realize, could take way longer than I anticipated.

"So, how has *your* Friday been?" I ask.

"Just fine," Alex says, sipping her Shirley Temple. "FCA met during lunch today, and—"

"FCA?"

"Fellowship of Christian Athletes," she clarifies. "For the past couple of meetings, Bernie and the FSM people have been coming by and trying to convert us with their stupid pamphlets. So we changed our meeting time, and now they won't be able to interrupt us again."

"Way to stand up for your principles," I say with a laugh.

Alex puts her glass down. "Excuse me?"

Only now do I realize what I've said, the awful way I said it. I think I just lost points.

"Oh," I say. "I just meant … I mean, you guys have every right to conduct your meeting without being interrupted. Why didn't you just tell FSM to take a flying leap? Now they've won, and you guys just look weaker."

She blinks at me. "Weaker?"

"Well, kind of, because you didn't stand up for yourselves."

"Weak*er?*"

"Exactly." And now I realize it. "Oh…."

Alex cocks her head at me like a hurt puppy. "You're … defending them?"

I look down into my water glass. I wish I could drown myself in there.

"I guess I was," I admit, "but I didn't mean to…."

"What did you mean?" she asks.

I pick up my head and look at her. "I just think that if you believe you're in the right, which you guys obviously do, you should say it—"

"What do you mean, 'you guys'?"

"—then you should man up and say it, and not just run away without a fight like a hypocrite!"

"Like a *hypocrite?*"

"Well, if the rosary fits…."

Alex looks at me like she's been shot. It's hanging in the air—what I

193

said, the awful way I said it, hanging in the air like a noose I've fashioned for myself. I didn't even mean to say it; I don't even know where it came from. But now it's out, and it's hanging there, and I'm pretty sure the humoring hour is over for both of us.

"What did you say?" she breathes.

"I said if the rosary fits. Look, I have nothing against athletes—nor do I have any personal stake in the goings-on of FSM—but I really don't blame them for going after you guys. I don't blame them one bit. I mean, what have you ever done for our school besides use sports as just another means for contributing to the boundary? You ostracize anyone whose beliefs don't align perfectly with yours! You reject choices and lifestyles that allow people to love whoever they want, live by whatever rules they want…." I look her in the eye. "Do whatever they want with their bodies…."

"Nobody should have the right to kill a baby, Max!"

"And nobody should have the right to regulate someone else's life choices! Did you know that unplanned pregnancy is the number-one reason why girls drop out of school? Screw pro-life, what about pro-education?"

"Yeah, what *about* education?" she says through gritted teeth. "I'm all for education! Here's your first lesson: rosaries are a *Catholic* thing, not a Christian thing. I'd like to think an 'educated' person like yourself would know that, but apparently you're too busy sitting up on your high horse, lumping every single religion together so you can hate more efficiently! Where did *you* get educated, at the Academy for Atheist *Douche Bags?*"

It's quiet. I glance at the next table over, where a couple sharing a breadstick plate is staring at us, and then cautiously back to Alex. She's red all over and trembling, and I wonder how many times she's actually been mad enough to say words like that out loud.

We sit very still, avoid each other's eyes. Alex stares at her Shirley Temple.

"What did you mean before?" she says gently. "'You guys' don't accept anything. What did you mean by 'you guys'?"

194

I thumb the edge of my water glass. "What did you mean by 'people like Bernie'?"

We look at each other. I'm trying so hard to think of something to say, to conjure some apology like a divine gift that will make everything good again. But I'm distracted by that gold cross of hers, twinkling at me under the stained-glass lamp as if to say, *I told you so.* I'm in a hell of my own making. I've taken Alex Lovett off her pedestal and put her into a box— and that's something I can't make up for with words.

I push away my water glass and say, "Screw this."

She raises her eyebrows at me.

"I went at this all wrong," I say. "I thought it'd be bitchin' to roll up in here like a big shot, but … I feel weird being here. Do you feel weird being here?"

Her blond hair bounces as she nods. "I keep expecting to run into my parents or something," she says.

"So screw this, let's get out of here!" I propose. "There's a McDonald's a couple blocks from here. I say we ditch this place, grab some cheap, shitty food, and just drive around, do whatever the hell we want. Whaddya say?"

She opens her mouth like she's going to agree, but then her near-full Shirley Temple catches her eye.

"It's OK; I got it," I say, rummaging around in my wallet. I fish out a five and smack it down onto the table. "Let's blow this joint."

Alex's shoulders fall, her gorgeous face brightens. "OK," she says with a smile, and we grab our jackets and head for my car.

* * *

"Turn left onto Fleet Street. Destination is on the left."

"That's Bridget, by the way," I explain to Alex as we pull into the Mc-Donald's parking lot. "She keeps me on track."

Alex chuckles. "It really is true—men will do anything to avoid asking for directions."

"Hey!" I retort. "That's a vicious, unfair stereotype!"

"Which happens to be legitimate," she says. "My dad has one of those things. My little brother and I change the language to German sometimes, just to mess with him."

"My, my, Miss Lovett," I gush. "And here I thought you were nice, sweet, pure of heart."

"It's an act," she says, and suddenly I'm grinning like a four-year-old.

The drive-through line is long, so we saunter inside and survey the menu. I've just decided what I want when a young-looking couple stumbles through the door and up to the cashier. The guy has super-short bleached-blond hair and a huge tattoo of a Venus flytrap up his arm. The girl's wearing a shirt that says, "Real men beat their meat, not their wives and children."

Right on time. I secretly suggested this particular McDonald's because it's a hot spot for stoners on weekend nights. Not that I know from experience. I've only smoked pot once and I didn't like it—I just got really uncomfortable and dizzy, and when I found out we didn't have any Pop-Tarts in the house I started crying. Since that pathetic episode, I haven't touched the stuff. But some people really seem to dig it—and those people tend to frequent this 24/7 establishment. Cheap food, free entertainment, what more could you want?

I nudge Alex in the elbow and nod at the stoners. They order their food efficiently, then lean against the wall and stare into each other's love-struck, puffy pink eyes. Guy Stoner clumsily reaches over and tucks a piece of Girl Stoner's mousy brown hair behind her ear. Then he clasps the back of her head and plants a huge, shameless kiss on her. Alex and I stare, fascinated.

"May I take your order?"

Neither Alex nor I have ordered because we've been watching the stoners neck. Alex snaps back into reality, places her order and pays the freckle-faced cashier. When I tell the cashier what I want, Alex shoves a stack of ones across the counter and says, "I got it."

I didn't expect this, and I guess it shows in my face. Alex smiles at me knowingly and says, "I owe you. For earlier."

Right about then, the stoners stumble back over to the counter to collect their to-go bags. Out of nowhere, Girl Stoner ogles Guy Stoner and says, "Look at us. It's like we're totally different …." They lock eyes. "But we're exactly the same!" They grab hands and traipse out the door, the distinct smell of weed and fry oil lingering in their wake.

Alex and I look at each other and crack up. The freckly cashier hands us our to-go bags, smiles slyly, and says, "You guys have a nice night."

We're still laughing by the time we get back on the main road.

"So, do you think that girl behind the counter thought we were …," Alex asks, unwrapping her cheeseburger.

"Stoned?" I say. "Naw. Potheads go in there all the time. That chick probably knows how to tell stoners from non-stoners like a reflex by now."

"That's why we used to go to Sonic," Alex says. "You don't even have to get out of your car."

"Yeah." I nod. "I could see how that would be the more logical choice—"

Wait.

I peer over my glasses at the darling of suburbia sitting next to me. "Are you saying that you … did you used to …."

She shrugs, grins at me, and bites into her burger.

"Alex," I stammer, "oh my God!"

"I know!" she says with her mouth full. She waves her hands and gulps. "Please, don't think any less of me for it—"

"I don't! I won't."

"I only did it a few times," she says. "The smoking, I mean. And I can see how it could be fun for some people … but not for me. Every time I did it I just got really paranoid and lazy, you know?"

"Yeah," I admit. "I know."

As we come to a stoplight, I realize I'm on a very different kind of date than I originally imagined. Alex has smoked pot. She's partaken in illegal

197

substances and doesn't seem to regret it one bit. What's weirder, she feels comfortable sharing this with me. What else will I learn about her before the night is over?

There's the hum of the engine, the muddled moans of Bruce Springsteen and the E Street Band on the radio.

"You're judging me," Alex says suddenly.

It takes me a second to realize the light is green. "What?"

"It's OK, I know what you're probably thinking," she calmly continues. "I've smoked marijuana, so I must not be such a strong Christian after all, right?"

I keep my eyes on the road and my mouth shut.

Alex shrugs. "I guess I just don't want you to think that I'm ... buttoned-up, or whatever." She looks out her window. "Or that ... *all* of us are buttoned-up. I mean, you know. It's not always the blind leading the blind. Some of us like to have fun." She looks at me. "You believe me, right?"

"Yeah," I decide. "I believe you."

"I mean," she continues, "not *all* Flying Spaghetti Monster people are misanthropic loud-mouths, right?"

"Whoa." I wag my finger at her. "Don't lump me in with Bernie and those whack-jobs. Those people are fucking crazy."

Alex throws back her head and laughs. "Is that a yes or a no?"

"I don't even know," I laugh. "So, Miss Cafeteria Christian, what kinds of stuff *do* you believe in? Public stoning of prostitutes?"

"Absolutely not," she asserts. "I have just as much sympathy for Paris Hilton as the next person."

"OK, what about heaven?"

"Yep."

"Gay marriage?"

"Go for it."

"Death penalty?"

"Sometimes."

198

"That's a yes."

She munches on a fry and nods. "I suppose it is."

"What about abstinence until marriage?"

We're swimming in dangerous waters now, and we both know it. It's quiet except for the ticking of the turn signal.

"I like the idea of it," she admits. "But I'm not sure it's … fair. I don't know if it's …"

"Realistic?" I venture.

"Yeah," she says. "Because …"

"Because no matter how nice some traditions look on paper, at the end of the day we're sexual beings with physiological needs, and there's no way to prettify that?"

She swallows. "Yeah. Something like that."

I let out a breath and smile to myself, amazed by how comfortable I am being out of my comfort zone.

"Max, where are we even going?" Alex asks, crumpling her burger wrapper into a ball.

I realize now that I have no idea. I haven't even paid any mind to Bridget since we left McDonald's; I've just been driving aimlessly.

"Well …," I don't want to suggest my place or hers, because I don't want this date to end. "You wanna go to the park? It's nice outside, we could swing!"

"OK!" she says, bouncing in her seat. "That sounds fun! I haven't swung in forever!"

I make a U-turn. Flint Park is close to our school, big and fenced-in to accommodate all the dog-walkers in our community. And even though I can't remember the last time I was there, as we power down the street with no semblance of a plan, I'm downright giddy. The streetlights blur by. Bridget's display screen goes dark. Van Halen comes on the radio, and when I reach out to adjust the volume at the same time Alex does, my fingers graze hers.

"Oh," I say stupidly, snatching my hand away.

"Go ahead," Alex says, hands folded in her lap. "I like this song."

So I turn up the volume, hoping she won't notice how shaky my hand is.

As we turn into the parking lot of Flint Park, a rogue raindrop splatters against my windshield. Then another. At first I think it might just be coming from the trees, but in no time at all a light but steady rain is coming down on us. "Dammit," I mutter as the swing set comes into view. By the time we pull into a parking space, it's become an all-out downpour.

"Well," Alex says, "that didn't pan out."

We both laugh. This whole *evening* hasn't panned out.

"It started really fast," I point out. "It might just blow through. Let's just wait a few minutes to see if it lets up."

"I dare you to go out there and hop on those swings anyway," she says.

"Fuck that!" I say. "I'm wearing Chucks—*you* go out there!"

"No way," she giggles, and locks her door. "I'm not going anywhere."

The rain's become so loud that I haven't even noticed what's on the radio until just now. A steady, tripped out baseline, John Lennon's unmistakable preacher-from-the-pulpit proclamations … it's "Come Together," my all-time favorite Beatles song.

"Oh my gosh!" Alex gushes. "I *love* this song!"

"I know, right?" I say, cranking the volume way up. "The best Beatles song *ever! Does anyone *not* love it?"

Alex attempts to sing along, stumbling her way through the first few nonsensical lyrics, until she gets to the first chorus.

"*I know yoooouuu,*" she croons, in a surprisingly sweet singing voice. "*You knooow meeee.…*"

I can't hold back. I jump in.

"*One thing I can tell you is you got to be free! Come together,*" we belt, "*right noooow … over me.*" I can't help but crack up, because I don't know if I've ever sung so candidly like this in front of someone before.

Alex catches her breath a second, then says, "That's my favorite lyric. I actually have it posted in the door of my locker."

I stop cold.

She looks at me and shrugs. "It inspires me," she explains.

Having been an atheist for most of my adolescence, I have never really understood the expression "leap of faith." I guess it's one of those things you don't really get until you do it.

"May I kiss you?" I breathe.

Alex locks eyes with me. Her chest rises and falls slowly beneath her shirt. There are no words between us—just the beat of the song, as driving as the rain.

The dim, yellow light of a streetlight outside bounces off that gold cross, vanishing just as quickly as it came. It's now or never. I kiss her.

It's soft at first, almost awkward. She's cautious. I put my hand on hers, stroke it a little to let her know I'm nervous, too, and I feel her relax against me. I try to readjust in the seat, get closer to her, but the fabric of my seat belt cuts into my neck.

"Sorry," I say, unbuckling my seat belt. "Maybe we should move."

With no grace whatsoever, I crawl over the armrest into the back seat, nearly smacking Alex in the face as I do. She unbuckles her own seat belt and clambers back with me. For the first time in a long time, she's not laughing.

We kiss again, and this time there's nothing cautious about it. Her fingers run through my hair and I shiver. I move my hands across her back, feel the softness of her skin, the sweat on the nape of her neck. I drag the tip of my finger down her spine and she gasps. She wraps her arms around me and we're enveloped in the sounds of the song, the pounding of the rain against the car, and all I can think about is how I have no idea what's happening, how I'm overwhelmed by the evolution of this unpredictable moment. This is the first time I've ever been OK with not knowing what's coming, with giving up control, with going forth on nothing more than a feeling. Is this what it's like to have faith?

I brush a strand of blond hair off her shoulder and kiss her neck. She whispers my name, and it feels just as good as I hoped it would. But then she pushes against my shoulder and says, "Max, wait."

I pull back from her and retract my hands. "Oh, my God, I'm sorry," I stutter. "I totally forgot. I mean, I didn't forget, I just—"

"Forget what?" she pants.

"That you're … you know …."

Alex rolls her eyes. "I already told you, Max. I'm not decided on the whole abstinence thing yet. I just think …"

I sit on my hands. "You shouldn't be … experimenting with someone like me?"

"No!" she says. "That's not it at all. I just … think this might be a little too fast for a first date."

I'm glad it's dark outside, because my face is probably red as hell. I adjust my glasses. "You're probably right," I concede.

"And I hate to say this," she adds, "but I've got a curfew."

"Oh, shit," I say, climbing into the front seat. "I totally forgot. Come on, let's beat it. I don't want to get you in trouble."

"No," she says, and she crawls over the armrest. "We wouldn't want *that,* would we?"

I grin and let my head fall against the headrest. Then I turn Bridget back on and stick the key in the ignition.

By the time we get to Alex's house, I still feel hot under my clothes. Fortunately, the rain has stopped.

"So," I say, walking Alex across her perfectly manicured front lawn. "What do we do now?"

She shrugs. "See you on Monday?"

"No." I shake my head. "Alex, what do we do … now. The two of us."

We stop when we come to her stoop. Alex sighs. "To be honest, I had an awesome time tonight." She digs into the grass with the toe of her shoe. "You're really cool, Max. But … I don't think I want to date you. I mean, do you really want to date me?"

I raise my eyebrows, suddenly feeling about four inches high. "No," I say, "I guess not."

"I just … I think we'd argue all the time," she reasons. "I think we'd kill each other!"

We both giggle. "Yeah," I agree, "maybe we would."

We're quiet for a second, listening to the night noises.

"It's late. I better go," she finally says. "I'll see you on Monday, then?"

"Yep, you'll see me," I say, shoving my hands in my pockets.

She flashes her brilliant smile at me and turns away. As I watch her climb the steps, I decide I'm not quite ready to stop being stupid.

"Hold on a sec," I say.

She turns around at the top of the steps.

"I lied," I confess. "I do want to go out with you again. And … I think you want to go out with me again, too, but I think we're both kind of … I don't know, scared."

She blinks at me. "Scared of what?"

"I don't know." I scratch my head. "Scared to make the leap?" I rock back and forth on the balls of my feet. "I mean, I know I am. 'Cause let's face it, you're no picnic."

Alex's mouth drops open. "What?" she says, bounding back down the steps. "*I'm* no picnic?" She grins and punches me in the shoulder. "That's just funny coming from you, Pious McSoapBox!"

"See?" I say. "You can't even keep your hands off me."

"I'm not even gonna dignify that with a response!"

"You just did, church girl."

"Ooh, nice one," she says. "Very creative. Original. Would you mind if I borrowed that for my superhero alter ego?"

"Well, I dunno," I say, stepping closer to her. "First you'd have to show me your superpowers."

Alex reddens, fast. "I will not tolerate these brazen overtures any longer," she teases. "You've ridiculed me, kept me up past my curfew, and now this conversation is officially over."

"No," I say, and I grab her by the wrist. "Seriously."

She looks at me hard for a second. Then she wraps her fingers around my wrist and gently removes my hand from hers.

"Let me think about it," she says softly. "I mean, you're right, but let me think about it."

She walks back up the steps, grabs the doorknob.

"I'll let you know on Monday," she says over her shoulder.

"I'll see you then," I say.

Alex smiles at me one last time, opens the door, and retires into her house. When I hear the click of the front door locking, I head back to my car.

I power up the car, turn the AC on full blast, and program Bridget to take me home. A soggy McDonald's bag on the floor catches my eye. Only now do I realize that Alex Lovett paid for my dinner tonight, and I still haven't touched it.

* * *

It's the weirdest Monday I've ever walked into.

I trudge through the junior hallway past the teachers taking bathroom breaks, past the hoards of students enjoying their five minutes of freedom between third and fourth period. A whole weekend has passed since my date with Alex, and that amazing feeling I had on Friday night seems totally irretrievable now. I don't know what I was thinking, suggesting Alex and I go out again. Sure, we can try—but I live in fear. I live in fear of saying the wrong fucking thing at the wrong time, like I did at Olive Garden. I live in fear of running out of things to talk about when there's no radio to fill the silence. But most of all, I fear looking into her eyes and remembering those few minutes in the back of my car—that line that we've already crossed. I don't think we can be alone together without that huge, Christian make-out elephant in the room as our chaperone.

I guess it doesn't really matter what I think, not if Alex decides she doesn't want to see me again. I haven't seen her around yet today, and

204

I'm starting to think she's avoiding me for that reason. Fine. See what I care. It'll be a relief, really. It'll be comforting to be back in the land of the familiar: I live in my little world, she lives in hers, and never the two shall meet. No more anxiety, no more fear; it really is the best course of action. I've come to terms with that.

I make it to my locker and let my book bag fall to the floor. When I go to put in the combination, I notice a small, folded piece of notebook paper taped to the dial. Someone has written *Max* on it in pink, flowery script. I open the note.

"As iron sharpens iron, so one man sharpens another."—Proverbs 27:17.

And then, below that:

Be my date for Godspell this Friday?—Church Girl.

Twenty lockers down, I see Alex closing her little metal door. She slings her backpack over her shoulders, straightens her hair. Then she smiles over at me, winks, and disappears into the science lab.

And just like that, I have a date for Friday night. I open up my locker, smooth out the note, and tape it to the inside of the door. Then I close my locker, pick up my bag, and head off to class.

Teddybear by Lydia Delp

V. Performing Childhood

Night Movie by Julie Blackmon

Snow Day by Julie Blackmon

Line-Up by Julie Blackmon

Concert by Julie Blackmon

Jean Stringam

Some Performance Notes

"My Joke About a Worm" is Cheyenne and Joaquin's rap from my young adult novel, *The Hoarders* (Springville, UT: Cedar Fort, 2010). Cheyenne and Joaquin are excited about a kid joke they believe will help them earn the money they urgently need. They sing this rap back and forth with a snap/clap beat. Then Joaquin starts to think about his mother in a little eight-bar melody. The older brother, Cheyenne, tries to keep the rap going, but soon joins Joaquin in wondering why she left them.

"All I Want" is Adele's song from the novel, *Balance* (Springville, UT: Cedar Fort, 2011). Adele is singing about what is important in her life. Some things make her happy to think about and some make her angry, so the music shifts back and forth. When you see note heads that look like a little "x" it means to speak the words in rhythm and more or less on pitch. (That's when she's angry.)

My Joke about a Worm

Rap by Cheyenne & Joaquin from THE HOARDERS

Jean Stringam

My Joke about a Worm

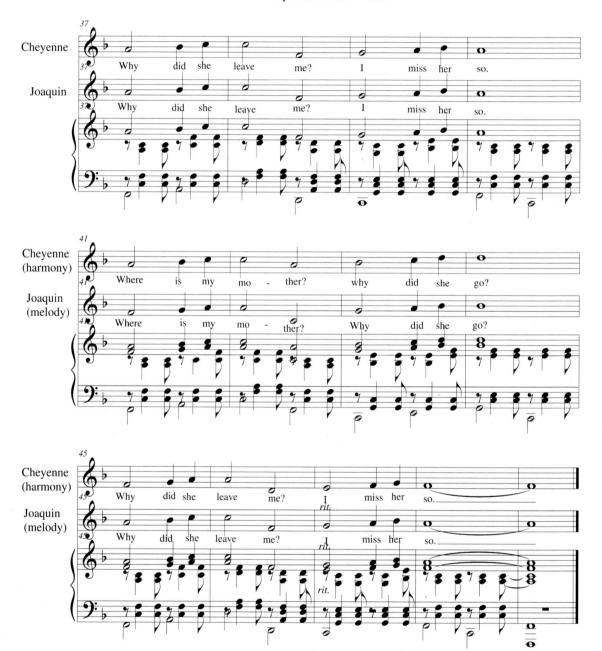

All I Want

Adele's song from BALANCE

Jean Stringam

Web pa - ges of my own, Girl - friends that I can phone.
Tell me when child - hood's done, Tell me grown up is fun.

All I want to be is a - bove all fam - 'ly quar - rels, Re - spec - ted, giv - en laur - els,
All I want to know is if a - ny - one has an - swers, If ad - mir - a - tion trans - fers,

Chic like my French au pair, Cool like my cou - sin's stare.
When should I stand a - part? Whom should I give my heart?

D.S. al Fine

All I want are so - cial

gra - ces, E - le - gance and pret - ty pla - ces, All I want is cool de - port - ment, Pro - per

words in wide as - sortment, All I want is calm and qui - et, Ta - ble manners? They should try it!

Teddybear by Jessica Stephenson

Renée Dunn

What to Say

Synopsis: A girl grapples with the death of her brother, assisted by his best friend and their memories.

Duration: 15-20 minutes

Cast: 5 (2 males, 3 females)

GAVIN: *17, Best friend of* WILL, *who was killed in a car accident*

CASEY: *16, Sister of* WILL

MOTHER: *of* WILL *and* CASEY—*Seen in flashbacks*

WILL: *17, Lip synchs most of his lines with* GAVIN *or* CASEY—*Seen in flashbacks*

MRS ANDERS: *Mother of an ex-girlfriend of* WILL's—*Seen in flashbacks*

Setting: Before a funeral. Stage right—Outside (minimal scenery—perhaps just a park bench) Stage left—empty space that flashbacks occur in.

Lighting note: There are three special light settings noted in the script. "Memory lighting" means lights are full on the left side. "Normal lighting" means lights are full on right side, and "Aside lighting" means that lights are one-half on the left, the flashback characters freeze, and lights are three-quarters on the right side. Center stage should remain dark as a demarcation between imagination/memory (L) and real time (R).

(GAVIN and CASEY are dressed in black for the funeral, and all other characters should be dressed in dark clothes, except for WILL, who should be in whites and grays. CASEY is seated R, picking at an unused Kleenex. As the play goes on she will continue to rip up pieces of the Kleenex whenever she is upset—resulting in a large amount of tissue confetti littering the floor by the end of the play. GAVIN is entering R as normal lights up.)

GAVIN: Hey.

CASEY: Hey. *(awkward hug) (long pause)*

GAVIN: So, they sent me out here to look for you.

CASEY: Yeah?

GAVIN: Yeah…. I don't think they know what to do with me.

CASEY: They don't know what to do with you? I'm living in a house with two zombies, that look a lot like our … my … parents. *(looks down and resumes picking at Kleenex)* I came out here to hide. I'm pretending I'm at the park.

GAVIN: Is it working? *(sits on bench next to CASEY)*

CASEY: Not so much.

GAVIN: How bad is it?

CASEY: Well…. *(stands) (fade into aside lighting)* When they asked me if I wanted to give a eulogy today I said no. In fact, *(crosses arms and walks to SL as lights fade into memory)* my exact words were, "Hell, no." *(MOTHER looks at CASEY without reaction and then nods and turns away. CASEY*

222

turns back—aside lighting—speaking to GAVIN *from across the stage, as though she is still near him)* My mom didn't even flinch.

GAVIN: Wow. She really is a zombie, huh?

CASEY: I said it on purpose. I just wanted to pretend like something was normal. I just wanted…. *(memory lighting)* (CASEY *reenacts posture/tone from previous line)*

CASEY: *(to* MOTHER*)* Hell, no.

MOTHER: Casey Marie! That is not how we speak to anyone and most certainly not how you speak to me.

CASEY: Sorry, Mom. *(lights return to normal as* CASEY *returns R)* I wanted that, you know. The normalcy. I wanted to be the rebellious daughter again, but I'm the sister of the boy who died—even to my mom. I'll never feel normal again, will I?

GAVIN: I don't know. I mean, I know eventually you and your parents … and all of the rest of us will find a new normal and we'll settle in again…. At least that's what everyone says. But I don't know if it will ever feel the same. I don't see how it could.

CASEY: There's a chipper thought. *(sits)*

GAVIN: I know. OK, so your parents have turned to zombies, and Will…. Well, what about you? How are….

CASEY: *(interrupting)* Let me just stop you right there…. I have a feeling you are about to ask me how I'm doing. Unfortunately I've made myself a pact that the next person who asks me how I'm doing is going to get a

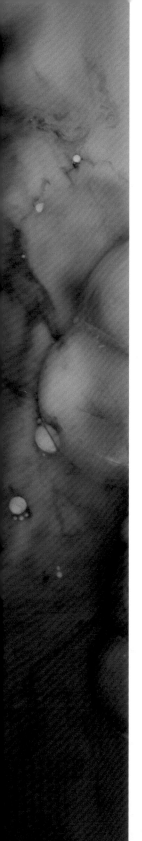

punch in the face. And considering you are giving a eulogy, it would be a shame to mess up that nice suit with stains from a bloody nose.

GAVIN: (*clearing throat*) Errrr … uh … no I wasn't going to ask that. (she looks at him suspiciously; he stands) I was going to ask how are … we … going to … convince … Elmo to run for mayor!

CASEY: (*laughs, halfheartedly*) Elmo? The red puppet? Well, I have to give you some props. At least that was a creative attempt.

GAVIN: (*getting warmed up now*) No, seriously, we need more Muppets in our government and you gotta start local if you wanna make it to the big time. Elmo's a sure bet. Kids love him, so moms will, too. And he's already got his own theme song, so that's awesome. Plus he knows Katy Perry and I bet he could get her to come down and campaign for him so you've got the male vote right there. I'm telling you, we gotta get him to run. It'll be the best thing this town has ever seen.

CASEY: You know you may have a point. Imagine the headlines. "Muppet for Mayor!" "Elect Elmo!" There is a lot of good alliteration in there, and everyone knows alliteration is how you get into office.

GAVIN: It's so true. And can't you just see Elmo dressed up in a suit? He'd totally knock them dead, don't … (*stops abruptly and looks at her panicked. She gets up and after a silent curse he does, apologizing*) I'm so sorry, Casey.

CASEY: (*quietly*) Don't, Gavin.

GAVIN: Don't … what?

CASEY: Don't do that.

224

GAVIN: I know, I'm sorry. I don't know what the heck is wrong with me, I just....

CASEY: No. Don't do that. Don't apologize for talking to me like a normal person. Don't start treating me like I'm made of tissues. Don't avoid every mention of death or dying or grief or sadness. Don't treat me like I'm Bella Swan and about to go into a living coma or ride a motorcycle off a cliff. And please don't pretend like you aren't hurting, too.

GAVIN: *(beat)* OK.

CASEY: Yes, he was my brother. Yes, we were close. But I don't know how to handle things any better than anyone else right now and if even you, his best friend, starts avoiding me and walking on eggshells around me because you don't want to say the wrong thing ... well, I might end up punching you in the nose after all.

GAVIN: Oh no! *(throws up hands)* Please don't punch me in the nose. I don't think I can withstand the gruesome fury of your girly little fist.

CASEY: *(laughs)* That's more like it.

GAVIN: *(pause)* Can I make a confession?

CASEY: Go for it.

GAVIN: I don't know what to say. I mean, not to you, we've established that ... but for the funeral. In twenty-five minutes. I'm really honored your mom asked and everything but ... I don't know what to say.

CASEY: Aren't you the captain of the debate team?

225

GAVIN: Yes, but this is a little different from giving a speech about why the U.S. should or should not explore space more, or even discussing if people have a moral obligation to help others in need. The answer is yes, by the way. This is a funeral. This is my best friend. This is saying good-bye … and I don't know what to say.

CASEY: Do you have any stories? That seems like a good thing to talk about … stories of crazy teenage antics? *(she sits)*

GAVIN: The only things I can think of make it sound like a roast. Like the other day I was coming over to play some video games …. *(lights fade to memory as GAVIN crosses, and WILL acts out what GAVIN speaks of)* As I was driving down the road I saw him doing this weird thing in the drive-way—looked like some crazy sort of rain dance. As I got closer, I saw that he had a cord in his hand and he was slamming something attached to it on the ground over and over. I got a little closer. It was a video game controller. He was out in the driveway smashing a controller into the concrete, 'cause he lost. He didn't stop until it was just a microchip attached to some wire. When I drove up he was standing there all out of breath *(GAVIN crosses his arms and looks at WILL)* and he just looked up, grinned, and said,

WILL: *(WILL's lips move but GAVIN actually says the line)* That'll teach it.

GAVIN: *(GAVIN crosses R as lights return to normal)* I laughed so hard. But, I'm not sure his temper is the most important thing to point out at his funeral, no matter how insane it was.

CASEY: That's where the other controller went….

GAVIN: Or there is the first time we met, and then subsequently got in a fistfight about whether the green Power Ranger or the black one was better.

226

CASEY: To be fair, you were both five, and you got over it … eventually. *(long pause; she stands and looks toward the funeral home R)* Did you see him in there?

GAVIN: Yeah.

CASEY: I've never seen a dead person before. Even all our grandparents are alive, still.

GAVIN: Me either. He looked … weird.

CASEY: Yeah. That color is…. Do you think they do that on purpose? Like the makeup people give them that awful color so that they don't look too alive, or do you think that's just the color that people are when they … aren't.

GAVIN: I don't know, but you're right. He looked wrong. Like a creepy wax sculpture of Will. And they put lipstick on him!

CASEY: *(laughs)* I know. He would have been so pissed. He would have smashed that lipstick on the ground until it was just a stick without any lip.

GAVIN: Well, it has it coming, being all pink-purple. *(looks up)* Not very manly, bro. Sorry.

CASEY: I think they call that mauve … in the lipstick biz.

GAVIN: Not being interested in the lipstick biz, I wouldn't know, but I can say that mauve was not mauve-alous.

CASEY: Something to remember to put in a will, someday. "To my heirs:

227

For the love of all that is holy, make sure they use a manly lipstick on me or else you get nothing."

GAVIN: I think I'll just get cremated so there isn't an issue.... *(sits)* So, was that Emily's mom talking to yours last night?

CASEY: Yeah, you aren't going to believe this. I was standing next to Mom so I heard everything she said.... *(looking stage left; memory lighting)*

MRS. ANDERS: I'm so sorry, Diane.

MOTHER: *(woodenly)* Thank you.

MRS. ANDERS: I can't believe it. Emily wanted to come tonight, but she just couldn't. The poor girl is beside herself. She's been a wreck since she first heard the news, sobbing uncontrollably. She loved him. She still loves him.

MOTHER: I'm sorry. *(aside lighting)*

CASEY: Can you believe that? The girl who cheated on Will, and then tried to convince everyone that he was the one who was cheating. The girl who called so often with hate messages that my parents had to block her number. She still "loves" him. Oh, and she's so upset that she couldn't come. Obviously, my parents aren't as upset as Emily, because I mean, they made it to the visitation. And then my mom apologized. Like it was all her fault that Will died and illustrated what a flipping nutcase Emily is.

GAVIN: That's sick.

CASEY: Oh wait, that's not all. After waxing on about what a wreck poor Emily is, Mrs. Anders said.... *(lights return to memory.)*

228

Mrs. Anders: Please let me know if there is anything I can do. If you need some help writing thank you notes or anything else.

Casey: *(lights return to normal.)* Of all the nosy, busybody, gossipy, looky-loo, total crap things to say. You know she just offered to do that so she could find out who sent us things, and somehow get in on the drama. That's when I made the "How are you doing?" pact with myself.... I was hoping she would come up to me and ask how I was doing and then I could punch her in the face. Unfortunately, she just smiled sadly at me and walked past.

Gavin: That's where that came from. I thought it was a pretty vehement reaction to a reasonable question.

Casey: It's not a reasonable question. How do they think I'm doing? I'm doing badly. I'm so pissed off. You really have no idea how good it would feel to punch someone's grandma right now. I just can't handle any more of it. The old lady perfume ... the sympathetic pats and the people who just stand there staring at you and holding your hand like that's going to do something. The tears ... and everyone's eyes! Even when they are keeping their distance everyone is looking at me, with the same eyes. The pressure is ... it's malicious! Everyone is waiting for me to break down. Everyone wants me to just dissolve into tears. But I'm not going to do it, damn it. And I don't want to be around all the people that want me to.

Gavin: *(stands)* Please, don't punch someone's grandma. If you need to punch someone now, go ahead and punch me. If you still have violent urges against little old women after the funeral, I'll set up a dartboard with a picture of Betty White in the center and you can go to town. And, Case, I don't think anyone wants you to break down. They probably just think it would be healthy.

CASEY: Well, they can shove healthy up their—

GAVIN: *(interrupting, in an imitation of her mother)* Casey Marie!

CASEY: *(grins)* Nose. *(Pause)* None of my friends will come near me. Are people treating you this way? You were his best friend. Are people treating you like you have swine flu?

GAVIN: Nah, Guys are tough, you know. So I'm getting a lot of long shoulder grabs or forearm clenches. Lots of "Sorry, man." Or sometimes the bro-hug. I know what you mean about the eyes, though. Feels like everyone is staring at me. Luckily, I've already broken down about three times so the pressure is off. *(pulls tissues out of suit jacket pocket)* I'm even carrying tissues around. I'm the most pathetic excuse for a tough guy ever.

CASEY: Tough guy? I repeat—aren't you the captain of the debate team?

GAVIN: Hey, James Earl Jones did speech and debate once upon a time. And you don't get tougher than Darth Vader.

CASEY: I dunno that he's such a bad ass. Wasn't he also the voice of a sweet and beloved Disney character?

GAVIN: A Lion King! He was a freaking lion king! I cannot believe you are questioning the manliness of James Earl Jones!

CASEY: Will would take my side.

GAVIN: Well, of course he would! But only because he liked to razz me. Not because he actually had any doubts as to whether or not James Earl Jones is a tough dude! Seriously, we had a conversation about this. *(lights*

230

fade to memory; GAVIN *crosses the stage, to where* WILL *is dribbling a basketball)*

GAVIN: *(to* WILL*)* Morgan Freeman or James Earl Jones? *(to* CASEY*)* And he said,

WILL: *(lip-syncing,* GAVIN *is actually the one speaking)* Are you kidding? James Earl Jones. *Field of Dreams! Lion King! Star Wars!*

GAVIN: *(to* CASEY*)* So, I said, *(to* WILL*)* OK, yes, but what does that have to do with which could win a pizza eating contest? *(to* CASEY*)* And then he said something so deep, so profound, so true, it will stay with me the rest of my life.

WILL: *(lip-syncing. Stops dribbling ball to look very seriously at* GAVIN*)* Dude. *(holds up first finger)* Darth. *(holds up second finger)* Vader. *(lights return to normal and* GAVIN *crosses back.)*

CASEY: Seriously? You count that as a conversation?

GAVIN: Did anything else need to be said? I mean, he established Jimmy Jones's dominance for all time in three words!

CASEY: *(laughs for a moment and then sobers)* Do you do this, too?

GAVIN: What?

CASEY: The highs and lows. Laughing and then yelling. Being sad and then joking around. I feel like a gremlin got inside my emotion controls and wrecked my system.

GAVIN: Well, a gremlin might explain your desire to pummel a grandma.

231

But, yeah, I do it, too. One second I want to be alone, one second I don't. There are only certain people I can stand to be around.

CASEY: It shouldn't have been him.

GAVIN: Yeah, we are way too young to die.

CASEY: No, *(sits)* I mean it should have been me. My entire life I've felt like I was going to die young. That I was headed for tragedy. That something terrible was going to happen to me so I had to live as much as I could, while I could. I've always lived with a sense of doom, and I was OK with that. I never really thought I'd make it to college. And now I find out.... It wasn't me. It was him.

GAVIN: Hey, don't worry, there is still time! *(CASEY just looks at him)* OK, wow, that was a really stupid thing to say. Are you sure that I shouldn't walk on a few eggshells? Cause I think you might hate me less when this is all said and done. *(sits)*

CASEY: Actually, it's kinda nice to watch someone insert their foot so fully in their mouth. I mean, I think your shoe is even still on it. Impressive.

GAVIN: Well, I'm not going to apologize, because that will land me in even more hot water. My pathetic attempt at humor aside, you know a lot of people have that feeling. It doesn't mean that it should have been you.

CASEY: Well, it sure shouldn't have been him! I wish I could trade places with him. He was so good, Gavin. So good. It sucked being his little sister sometimes, 'cause I could never live up to him. He always got better grades than me, he was always better liked by his teachers, heck, I think Mom and Dad even liked him better most days ... not that they'd ever admit that. He was a golden boy. I started picking what I was going to do

232

in high school based solely on what he wasn't doing. And trust me, those pickings were slim. I don't even know if I like business classes … he just didn't take them. And now he's gone … and I can't live up to that. How am I supposed to be their golden boy? I'm a girl and I like silver. But I feel so guilty for being alive. I was prepared to die. I wasn't prepared to live.

GAVIN: You know it wouldn't be any different if it was you in there and me out here with him, right? He'd be talking about you like you were this perfect sister….

CASEY: Are you implying I'm not a perfect sister? *(puts up her fists)*

GAVIN: *(smiles and jokingly responds)* Oh, not in the least … you are a paragon of brains and spunk and heart.

CASEY: *(smiles)* That's what I thought.

GAVIN: I'm saying that he would be glossing over the time you put peanut butter in his toothpaste or told your mom that he was lying about staying with me so he could try and spend the night with Emily. Good call on that one, by the way.

CASEY: Yeah, no kidding. Glad she didn't get her psycho-hooks any further in him than she did.

GAVIN: He wasn't perfect. But I notice you haven't mentioned all the times he wrestled you to the ground and sat on you until you let him get his way. Or the time he stole your journal and we acted out all the best scenes from it during your slumber party.

CASEY: *(narrows her eyes)* I'd forgotten about that. You still owe me for that one.

GAVIN: It's been three years. Statute of limitations has passed, my friend.

CASEY: Am I?

GAVIN: Are you…?

CASEY: Your friend?

GAVIN: Well, yeah, Casey. I mean, I've spent just as much time at your house as I did at my own since I was five years old. Your brother was my best friend, and as you pointed out, not so long ago, you two were close. How could you not be my friend? You probably know more about me than anyone else in the world … at least, now.

CASEY: Well, it was always you and Will. I just tagged along.

GAVIN: Yeah, but after a few years, it stops feeling like tagging along and it starts feeling like … normal…. *(checks watch)* Hey, we gotta get in there. It's starting soon.

CASEY: But, you didn't figure out what to say.

GAVIN: Actually, I did, kinda. I'm telling the Darth Vader story … and the controller story, and probably the Power Ranger fistfight story. Cause … it's better if I talk about him the way that he was, you know? Real. With flaws … and still the best friend I ever had. And if you don't mind, I'll throw in a few stories about the two of you. *(she nods)* You know … you guys used to make me jealous and wish I had a sibling.

CASEY: Well … *(she smiles sadly)*

GAVIN: Yeah…. *(hugs CASEY)* Come on.

CASEY: Go ahead. I'll be right behind you. I just need a sec.

GAVIN: (looks at her) You sure? (she nods, and he puts his arm around her neck and pulls her in for another hug and kisses the top of her head) OK, but I'm not letting any grandmas come out to check on you, just so you know.

CASEY: (she shoves him gently) Go. (GAVIN exits R)

(Lights fade to memory, WILL enters)

WILL: (lipsynching as CASEY speaks for him) Hey, Case, you don't need the car for anything tonight, do you?

CASEY: Nah, I have homework I have to get done. Geometry is killing me. (throws him the keys)

WILL: (lipsynching as CASEY speaks for him) Great! I'm headed over to Gavin's. Will you tell Mom and Dad when they get in? (she nods) You're the best kid sister a guy could ask for! (he heads out)

CASEY: (she calls after his retreating back) I'm your only sister … and sixteen months' difference doesn't make me a kid! (she stares after him for a while and then turns R to leave, and WILL comes back into the light.)

WILL: (speaking in his own voice) Hey, Case? (she freezes and slowly turns) I'll miss ya. I love you, you know. (WILL waves and exits L)

CASEY: (lights return to normal as CASEY starts to cry) I know.

Lights fade out.

Ken Gillam and Shannon R. Wooden

Horror and the Horrible Child
in Pixar's *Toy Story* (1995)

The Pixar animation studios indisputably house some of the cleverest
minds in contemporary cinema. The films, in addition to their incompa-
rable animation, award-winning music, and rich, multivalent stories, are
peppered with visual puns, innocuous but adult jokes, and intertextual
"Easter eggs" planted in their rich and colorful backdrops. In *Toy Story 2*
(1999), for instance, Rex's attempt to catch up to his friends in the Barbie
car recalls a terrifying scene from *Jurassic Park* (1993); Hamm's reference
to Woody's "laser envy" in the first film surely elicits a chuckle from
viewers at least minimally familiar with the theories of Sigmund Freud.
These subtle, often tongue-in-cheek additions may seem immaterial
to the task of interpreting the films: Mr. Potato Head's rearranging his
features and saying, "Look, I'm a Picasso," doesn't necessarily compel a
comparative reading of the film with Modernist art. But graphic elements
can be crucial to character development, as in the case of Sid Phillips, a
character marked as the bully-villain of *Toy Story* (1995) visually as much
as he is narratively. The visual and narrative messages of children's films,
as scholars have noted, may be ideologically influential, even "pedagog-
ical," shaping the way viewers read not only the films themselves but the
culture in which they perform (Giroux 10). Particularly in a children's
film like *Toy Story,* which unambiguously asks its child viewers to fear
and detest another child, we believe it is worthwhile to analyze how
such visual characterization works to classify some children as protagonists and others as villains. What we discover under Sid's frighteningly
drawn surface is a conventional horror trope, hidden in plain sight on
the unique ontological landscape of the film, and, subsequently, a rather

236

alarming means of defining and disciplining those behaviors and traits the film deems evil.

Some of the visual coding that Pixar uses to vilify Sid is as simple as the Wild West narratives that Andy plays out in his Technicolor room. The good child wears a clean, colorful or white shirt, shorts, and, often, a bright red cowboy hat; Sid's black T-shirt sports a skull eerily congruent with his close-cropped head. Andy's walls are painted baby blue with puffy white clouds; Sid's space is darkly paneled, celebrating death metal music with posters of bands like Wraith Rock Monster, Kill'n Paul Bunyan and his Blue Ox of Doom, and Megadork. Andy's face is open, his expression placid, bright eyes wide. Sid's expressions, on the other hand—he snarls, he leers, he cackles maniacally—remain as intense and serious as his imaginative roles require: he does, after all, work in military intelligence, aeronautics, and neurosurgery. His face itself—often presented in close-up, at least once literally magnified in a glass—features arched eyebrows, squinted green eyes, and gigantic, metallic, almost predatory teeth so prominent he can barely close his lips over them. The close-up technique itself contributes to Sid's negative depiction, regularly positioning the viewer not only in proximity to but beneath Sid, simultaneous with the small, vulnerable objects of his gaze. Supported by this visual context, the narrative needs only a gesture to reinforce Sid's badness (he "tortures toys," Rex cries), before viewers are fully educated in how to read him.

Viewers are thus visually guided through the narrative tension of one of the film's main storylines. While certainly, on the one hand, *Toy Story* explores the rivalry between the principal toy characters, ultimately teaching a lesson of cooperation and empathy, on the easily-visualize-able other hand, the film also documents the abduction, captivity, and escape of two little toys from a violent, even sociopathic predator who abducts innocents from a neighborhood pizza arcade. The message comes through clearly: scholars and fans alike consistently refer to Sid as "disturbed," "sadistic," "evil," even "psychotic" (see Byrne and McQuillan

237

127; fansite http://disney.wikia.com). In this light, *Toy Story* appears as an infantilized analogy of *Law and Order: SVU* (1992-2012), its suspense arising from the imagined terror of the powerless faced with a figurative kidnapper quite literally threatening bodily harm.

More precisely, though, the film tells a horror story, not only imbuing Sid with frightening traits but associating him with the monstrous. Noel Carroll, in *The Philosophy of Horror* (1990), explains how works of art horror do not merely generate fear of something dangerous, but "compound" threat with "revulsion, nausea, and disgust" by challenging prevailing notions of purity and taxonomy (22). Situated between life and death, between human and animal, even between man and machine, the "monsters" of horror are "categorically interstitial, contradictory, incomplete, and/or formless … not classifiable according to our standing categories" (34, 33). Horror is cognitively disruptive, "cross[ing] the boundaries of the deep categories of a culture's conceptual scheme" (31-2). Sid's house does indeed represent a dangerous space for Woody and Buzz—even falling into his yard is fatal to the Combat Carl blown to smithereens in Sid's first appearance—and his destructiveness may reasonably inspire fear in his toy captives, posing as it does an imminent threat to them. But it is also, in Carroll's definition, horrifying. He does not simply damage toys, he reconstructs them, and he does so in categorically contradictory ways. Scuttling out from beneath bedroom furniture in an eerie, silent greeting, Sid's menagerie of mutant toys exemplifies the categorical impurity that defines the monstrous. In Sid's taxonomically impure workshop, categories of age-appropriateness, commercial type, and even species have no meaning: baby noisemakers and dolls blend with the robotic or militaristic; humanistic body parts are grafted onto animals, tools, or machines. Sid breaks stuff, certainly, but he has also created more monsters than Victor Frankenstein ever imagined.

Carroll argues that in works of horror "the emotional reactions of characters … provide a set of instructions or, rather, examples about the way we are meant to react to the monsters in the fiction" (17). Buzz's and

Woody's reactions to Sid's mutants thus teach an unambiguous lesson about how to read the categorically impure: even other toys are both fearful and repulsed by the altered playthings, with Woody calling one a "disgusting freak" and Buzz literally proposing violence, changing his laser setting "from stun to kill." Two other scenes in the film similarly model revulsion as the appropriate response to the interstitial. When Sid returns his sister Hannah's doll, Janie, having replaced her head with that of a toy pterodactyl, Hannah recoils in utter horror. Nothing indicates that she fears for her own physical safety, even at the hands of her toy-vivisectionist brother. His physical gesture is not one of aggression but of offering, if tauntingly so, and his offering, however altered, is not a weapon but a toy. Still, her reaction conveys neither anger at having had her toy mutilated nor sadness at losing a favorite plaything. Instead, her impossibly wide eyes riveted to the altered toy, she shrieks in horror and flees, less from Sid than from the dinosaur-head doll he wields. Similarly, though Andy's toys are always aware of the possibility of breaking, losing, or interchanging their parts (hosting seminars on things like "what to do if you, or a piece of you, is swallowed"), the playroom gang, like Hannah, is more horrified than fearful when Woody waves Buzz's dismembered arm through Sid's window. Separated by the chasm between suburban houses and the impossibility of crossing the divide unaided, Woody poses no actual threat to the toys still at Andy's house. Besides, it would appear from Buzz's experience that a toy can lose an arm without suffering pain or loss of life. Woody himself is no more horrified to discover Buzz's injury than the whole gang will be in *Toy Story 3* (2003) when Mrs. Potato Head's lost eyeball gives them a kind of satellite access to the playroom. But the fact of Buzz's hand being waved by Woody's arm—suddenly neither Buzz's nor Woody's but situated in between—fundamentally challenges the gang's conceptual scheme. Rex vomits, concretely exhibiting that revulsion and disgust with which horror compounds any fear of threat. From this monstrous example, the gang is, at least momentarily, convinced of the honorable lawman's having become an evildoer.

The film ultimately rehabilitates Woody's reputation and reveals the basic decency of Sid's mutant toys, perhaps tacitly teaching its viewers that they should look beneath the surface before judging a person's character. Sid, however, remains unforgiven. He gets punished, viciously, by means of a meticulously organized climactic plot to combine the fear, revulsion, and cognitive disruption of horror, complete with a visual homage to one of the scariest horror films of all time.

Sid's Frankentoys, like art-horror monsters, may defy category, but nothing in the film is as potentially cognitively disruptive as its foundational fantasy: toys are alive. In a fantastic realm, where, as Carroll describes, the extraordinary is presented as ordinary (16), it is normal for Potato Head dolls to see through dislocated eyeballs and for pull-string cowboys to have crushes on plastic Bo Peeps. But the film world is not simply fantastic; in Andy's world, a world of birthday parties and yard sales, such fantastic things are inconceivable. The film has it both ways, superimposing the fantastic onto the recognizable real, and the main characters navigate the liminal space between fantasy and realism as a fundamental part of the film's plot. Pursuing their narrative quests with the added difficulty of remaining unseen, the toys understand the cognitive patterns that separate their realm from the human world and observe the distinction without question, even putting themselves in harm's way rather than betraying their sentience to humans.

The audience's engagement with the film's multivalent ontological construction is richly complex. Members of the audience—even the smallest children—understand on some level that they are watching a fantasy, and must, even as they suspend disbelief, realize that their world more closely resembles Andy, Sid, and Hannah's than Buzz and Woody's, and that the nature of existence they actually hold to be true is the humans', not the toys'. Even so, the structure of the narrative places Woody and Buzz at its center, where they can become the characters with which the audience is likely to identify. Viewers are further tied to Woody and the other inhabitants of the fantastic realm through the inescapable dramatic irony on which the whole film is built: they know what the toys know, even though other humans do not. Through willing suspension of disbelief and the functional muteness of the cinematic viewer, audience members become complicit, even intimate with the toys throughout their adventures and travails.

From this position, horror may seem a narratively fitting end to Sid's reign of horrifying others. Furthermore, this ontological construction is essential to his come-uppance. It is not Sid, after all, who transgresses the ultimate boundary to become the film's climactic monster. Revealing himself to Sid as a sentient being, Woody not only violates the cardinal rule of toys but his ontological category in the human world to become something more influential in that realistic realm, and if such a cognitive disruption is not horrifying enough, Woody punctuates his threats by spinning his head around like the demonically possessed Regan in *The Exorcist* (1973). The plan, of course, works perfectly. For Sid, a moment of happily playing in his yard turns to one of abject horror: his toys are alive, furious, and threatening constant surveillance for the rest of his life.

Sid's horrified reaction is of a piece with other horror reactions in the text, but his horror, instead of teaching viewers how to respond to the horrific, teaches the audience that certain children deserve this kind of punishment. In the contrast between Andy and Sid, the good child and the bad one, *Toy Story* defines this certain blameworthy child and thus tacitly reveals an ethics of boy culture. Conventional wisdom says that Sid is a bully, but in fact, the multivalent ontological situation underpinning the climactic, cognitively transgressive assault on Sid is equally necessary to his narrative status as a villain in the first place. In a purely fantastic realm, the claim of Sid's bullying would be unproblematic enough: Ursula the sea witch, for instance, is a fantastic bully, angrily and resentfully wielding power over other denizens of Disney's *The Little Mermaid's* (1989) fantastic landscape. But a purely realistic perspective would fail entirely to draw Sid's behavior as bullying. In a realistic world, Sid's just a kid who spends a lot of time alone in his room, who is delighted to

241

get an extra prize from a vending machine, who plays with his dog and teases his sister but never does anyone physical harm. In order to see Sid as a bad boy who gets his just desserts, we must believe two things: one, toys can suffer fear pain, even death; and two, *Sid doesn't know this.* He has to be surprised—his cognitive schema disrupted—in order to be appropriately punished for his crime, but if he is surprised, his crime can't have been intentionally committed. In practical terms, then, Sid's horrific punishment is earned not by bullying but by the nature of his play.

What we actually know about Sid, uninterpreted by the toys who fear him, is pretty simple: one, he enjoys minimal amounts of supervision. The only adult discourse directed to him is when his mother yells, from off-screen, that his "Pop Tart is ready." When we see (presumably) Sid's father, he is reclined in front of the television in the middle of the day, a pile of empty cans next to his armchair. Neither parent seems to know or care about even his most age-inappropriate experiments and acquisitions, like the rocket he straps to Buzz, advertised as "extremely dangerous" and unsuitable for children. Though she doesn't answer, Sid even asks his mother where to find matches, further suggesting a certain lack of engaged parenting. Sid also keeps numerous deadbolts on his bedroom door, for some reason deliberately shutting his family out. Secondly, we know that Sid doesn't get along with his sister. Many viewers read their interaction as evidence of his bullying, but a quick review of Hannah's behavior points more plausibly to sibling rivalry: unafraid of her brother, she taunts as she is taunted and is only too happy to co-opt his toy for her play, altering Buzz to be Mrs. Nesbitt. She delights in adding to his terror after his horrific confrontation in the yard, chasing him upstairs with her doll. Third, thanks to an Easter egg in *Toy Story 3,* we know he's on a path to being the garbage man, literally picking up the trash Andy discards as he packs for college, suggesting that whatever punishment he warrants in this film he will pay across a life trajectory, or at least an entire trilogy.

We also know that he doesn't "play nice" with toys. The film allows a little latitude in seeing rough play as typical, at least among boys. Though

242

the film visually marks Sid and Andy as binary opponents, they are not wholly dissimilar in their play. Both children anthropomorphize toys and invent detailed narratives to enact; both children's narratives incorporate elements of antagonism. Interestingly, it is Andy, not Sid, who makes his toys imitate violent and antisocial behaviors: they rob banks, rustle sheep, threaten violence, and shoot each other with lasers. Sid's ostensibly violent stories actually recount Mission Control's preparations for launching a rocket into space, a doctor's performing experimental surgery. The film even permits genuine, non-play antagonism, within imaginative parameters, anyway: Woody, tacitly likening himself to Sid, admits that he'd like to see Buzz like Combat Carl, "as a crater," and his sentiment, if only by its personal, jealous motive, may actually be meaner than the behavior Sid demonstrates, which is, in Rex's words, "just for fun."

Motive aside, however, Sid deliberately breaks stuff, and that seems to be his unpardonable sin. Perhaps the biggest difference between *Toy Story's* definitions of good boy and bad is that Sid sees toys impersonally, as largely de-identified objects that may be manipulated, destroyed, or repurposed in the name of play. Andy, even when playing rough, identifies toys mainly according to their prescribed commercial role. Though Potato Head gets to play the role of Black Bart, Sheriff Woody is always Sheriff Woody, Buzz Lightyear is always Buzz Lightyear, and Slinky Dog, though sometimes a "force field attack dog," still basically functions as a dog. In Sid's world, by contrast, Janie is just a plastic body on which to install a pterodactyl head, and a jack-in-the-box can as effectively house a disembodied hand as a jack. To Sid, Buzz is a nameless "spaceman," and since he has "always wanted to put a spaceman into orbit," this toy works narratively better than most. Sid, in other words, lacks a certain respect for the marketed identity of the commercial product. As Eleanor Byrne and Martin McQuillan argue, in *Deconstructing Disney* (1999), "Any interference within the commodity and its value is a challenge to the chain of production and is figured as a psychosis.... [Sid's] disrespect for brand labels and the singularity of merchandising is an affront to the global entertainment complex" (127). Sid's badness may be ascribed to his failing to honor the commodity, ignoring the commercial context that defines his toys as personalities, and refusing to preserve the integrity of the mass-marketed product. Woody is explicit about what Sid must do to redeem himself, if his injunction begs one important question: "From now on," he warns, "you must take good care of your toys!"

"Good care" in *Toy Story* carries an emotional component as well as a physical one. As he fails to preserve the bodily integrity of toys, Sid likewise fails to emotionally attach to his toys. Since he generally plays with one at a time (and, given the rate of his destructive games, often not the same one twice), his toys never appear to him as a community. They bear no real relation to one another and no relation to him. Andy's toys, on the other hand, comprise a tight-knit community, all committed to loving and supporting their child. Though Andy cannot know of their stated devotion to him, he does see them as entities with whom he maintains a loving relationship. He gives Woody rides on his shoulders, hugs Buzz and Woody closely, and grieves (or at least pouts) when they get damaged or lost. Probably not believing that his toys are alive, Andy still treats them as beloved personal objects—and individual characters, if not actual people. Even surrounded by his playthings, Sid remains wholly alone.

Sid's badness may then arise in part from his difficulty imagining and sustaining affectionate, nurturing relationships. In the context of the Pixar catalog, this explanation seems highly plausible: to fulfill his narrative destiny, Lightning McQueen, in *Cars* (2006), must choose to honor his surrogate father rather than win his big race; Mr. Incredible of *The Incredibles* (2004) has to realize that he needs the support and talents of his wife and children to be truly incredible; Sully of *Monsters, Inc.* (2001) must put saving a child before his professional ambitions; even Buzz Lightyear himself learns to reject his macho branded status to earn his place in Andy's heart. As we have previously argued, Pixar regularly punishes boys flying solo, bringing them each in line, ultimately, with a more self-effacing set of values that support the community and family (Gillam and Wooden 2). Sid, it would seem, rejects the social and emotional value of community building.

To a cocky alpha race car unable to sustain friendships or an egotistical superhero unable to connect to his family, maybe such discipline rings differently than to a poorly socialized, unsupervised, even neglected, boy, playing roughly, if typically, with toys. And finally, in many ways, Sid is not typical at all. It is perhaps no coincidence that Carroll calls filmic monsters, inspiring fear and repulsion in those around them, "disturbances of the natural order … extraordinary character[s] in our ordinary world" (16). Clearly gifted with mechanical ability and intense focus, Sid is far from ordinary. It is not every child who can rebuild an entire playroom's worth of toy parts. It is tongue-in-cheek, maybe, that he role-plays both as "rocket scientist" and "brain surgeon." But it is shockingly common for highly gifted children, curious, inventive, and experimental, to be "seen by others as different and out-of-step" (Webb et al. 14, 27).

Further, Sid is exuberant in his imaginative play, if not warm and empathic for family, friends, or anthropomorphic toys. Not a sociopathic predator driven by anger, hatred, or violent tendencies, Sid plays with intensity, skill, creativity, and joy. Indeed, when Buzz first sees Sid, he calls him "that happy child," only to be immediately disciplined by his own community into deriding and fearing the already isolated boy, even as they all acknowledge that he behaves as he does "just for fun." Scholars of gifted education have long warned that highly gifted and talented students may struggle with social interaction, having difficulty making friends with peers, failing to be understood and nurtured appropriately by adults (Webb et al. 171). If not punishing a typical boy for rough but perfectly typical play, could Pixar itself be bullying extraordinary boys?

Considering Pixar's other gifted engineers and inventors—from Syndrome *(The Incredibles)* to Charles Muntz *(Up!,* 2009) to Flik the Ant *(A Bug's Life,* 1998)—another surprising pattern emerges, a pattern that always vilifies or ridicules extraordinary intellect, inventiveness,

245

and mechanical ability, valuing only subordination to a community's or family's needs. The pattern is no doubt ironic, given the indisputably extraordinary technological minds at Pixar, but with so many examples, it is nonetheless hard to ignore. Nor is it a message in a vacuum, according to studies that make the garbage man trajectory seem downright mean. Many highly gifted children, scholars warn, "through early neglect or frustration, or through later choices that trap them … defy the society which does not seem to understand or accept them," dropping out, underachieving, battling depression or drug addiction, and otherwise falling far short of the potential they seemed to have as children (Streznewski qtd. in Fiedler 181).

Giroux argues compellingly that "media culture has become a substantial, if not primary, educational force in regulating the meanings, values, and tastes that set the norms that offer up and legitimate particular subject positions" (2). Pixar has been lauded and criticized for its host of male protagonists, at least until *Brave* (2012); but it seems clear that across the Pixar canon only a certain type of boyhood has been celebrated. A value system for boy culture begins to emerge in this very first feature film, visible in the contrast between the beloved Andy and the vilified Sid. Whatever comprises Sid's unpardonable offense, finally—whether we should read him as anti-commercial, anti-social, or simply exceeding the relatively narrow realm of so-called normalcy, thinking differently about how things work—it behooves us to interrogate the lessons we, and our kids, are being taught. "Not innocent," says Giroux, the culturally powerful messages of Disney "must be interrogated for the futures they envision [and] the values they promote" (7). The brilliance of Pixar also renders it uniquely pedagogically powerful to a post-feminist generation of children.

Works Cited

Byrne, Eleanor and Martin McQuillan. *Deconstructing Disney*. London: Pluto P, 1999. Print.

Carroll, Noel. *The Philosophy of Horror, or Paradoxes of the Heart*. New York: Routledge, 1990. Print.

Fiedler, Ellen D. "Advantages and Challenges of Lifespan Intensity." *Living With Intensity*. Ed. Susan Daniels and Michael M. Piechowski. Scottsdale, AZ: Great Potential Press, 2009. 167-84. Print.

Gillam, Ken and Shannon R. Wooden. "Post-Princess Models of Gender: The New Man in Disney-Pixar." *Journal of Popular Film and Television* 36.1 (2008): 2-8. Print.

Giroux, Henry A. *The Mouse That Roared: Disney and the End of Innocence*. Lanham, MD: Rowman and Littlefield, 1999. Print.

Toy Story. Dir. John Lasseter. Walt Disney Pictures and Pixar Animation Studios, 1995. Walt Disney Video, 2001. DVD.

Webb, James T., Janet L. Gore, Edward R. Amend, and Arlene R. DeVries. *A Parent's Guide to Gifted Children*. Scottsdale, AZ: Great Potential Press, 2007 Print.

Notes on Contributors

YOUNG E. ALLISON (1853-1932), born in Henderson, KY., became editor of *Henderson News* (Evansville, IN) and the *Courier-Journal* (Louisville, KY). The author of *On the Vice of Novel-Reading* (1897), *Delicious Vice* (1907-09), and *Curious Legend of Louis Philippe in Kentucky* (1924), Allison is chiefly remembered for the poem "Derelict," which he wrote to complete the verse fragment "Fifteen Men on the Dead Men's Chest," which appeared in Robert Louis Stevenson's *Treasure Island* (1883).

DONNA BARKMAN, an adjunct faculty member at the Bank Street College of Education in Manhattan, is a poet and short-play playwright, performing her own work and that of others, and specializing in ekphrastic poetry that is presented in galleries and museums in the New York City area. Her work has been published in *Chautauqua, The Westchester Review, ragazine.cc, Per Contra,* and *String Poet.* She has enjoyed two residencies in Wyoming—at the Jentel Artist Residency Program and at the Brush Creek Foundation for the Arts.

JAMES S. BAUMLIN, an editor of Moon City Press, is professor of English at Missouri State University. He has published extensively in Seventeenth-Century English literature, the history of rhetoric, critical theories, composition, and writing pedagogy.

ELEANOR LEONNE BENNETT, a sixteen-year-old photographer from the United Kingdom, has won awards for her work from *National Geographic,* the World Photography Organization, Nature's Best Photography, Papworth Trust, Mencap, The Woodland Trust, and Postal Heritage. Her photographs have been published in the *Telegraph, The Guardian,* and the BBC News Website and have appeared on the covers of books and magazines in the United States and Canada. Her art has been exhibited in Los Angeles, Florida, Washington, London, Paris, Indonesia, Scotland, Wales, Ireland, Canada, Spain, Germany, Japan, and Australia.

Noted photographer JULIE BLACKMON was born in Springfield, MO, where she works and lives with her family. She studied art at Missouri State University, where she developed an interest in photography. She has won numerous awards for her photographs, which frequently focus on family dynamics and children in order to "move beyond the documentary to explore the fantastic elements of our everyday lives." Her work is part of many permanent collections, such as those of the Kemper Museum of Contemporary Art, the Museum of Fine Arts (Kansas City, MO), the George Eastman House (Rochester, NY), the Museum of Fine Arts (Houston), and the Photographic Center (Seattle). She has published in many magazines, including *The New Yorker, Time, Vanity Fair* (Italy), *The New York Times Magazine,* and *Oxford American. Domestic Variations,* a monograph of her work, was released in 2008.

JOEL D. CHASTON is distinguished professor of English at Missouri State University, where he teaches children's and young adult literature. A past president of the Children's Literature Association, he has published several scholarly books and edited collections, including *Bridges for the Young: The Fiction of Katherine Paterson* (with M. Sarah Smedman), *Lois Lowry,* and *Theme Exploration: A Voyage of Discovery.* A former assistant editor of *Children's Literature Association Quarterly,* his essays have appeared in many journals, including *Children's Literature Association Quarterly, The Lion and the Unicorn, Children's Literature in Education,* and *Five Owls.*

JOE COVER has a Master of Arts in Creative Writing and teaches at Missouri State University and Ozarks Technical Community College. He has published short fiction in *Straylight* and *Moon City Review* and poetry in the *Haiku Journal*. He lives with his inspiration, his loving wife, in a ninety-year-old-house in rural Missouri.

RENÉE DUNN earned her bachelor's degree at Missouri State University in 2006. She was a high school speech and theater teacher for two years, and uses that experience to write for the students she once taught. She currently does contract work for children's video games and hopes to begin a MA in the fall of 2012. She also posts daily on her blog (www.minusambition.blogspot.com), where she relates her thoughts and experiences on a myriad of topics, from young widowhood to nail polish.

JACEK FRACZAK, an assistant professor in the Department of Art and Design at Missouri State University, received his Master of Fine Arts from the Academy of Fine Arts (Warsaw, Poland).

KEN GILLAM is an assistant professor and composition director in the English Department at Missouri State University. In 2008, he and Shannon Wooden published their first article on gender and Pixar films, which has been anthologized in *The Gendered Society Reader* and *Men's Lives*. Composition theory and pedagogy along with cultural rhetorics comprise his research interests.

D. GILSON is a Ph.D. candidate at George Washington University and holds an MFA from Chatham University. An alumnus of Missouri State University, his work has appeared in *The Los Angeles Review, PANK, The Rumpus,* and in his chapbook, *Catch & Release,* which won the 2011 Robin Becker Prize. His website is dgilson.com.

The Boy With a Drum (1969), the first children's book by DAVID HARRISON, eventually sold over two million copies. In 1972, Harrison gained national recognition when he received the Christopher Award for *The*

Book of Giant Stories. Since then, he has published seventy-seven original titles, which have sold more than fifteen million copies and has earned numerous honors. His writing has been anthologized in more than one hundred books and has been translated into twelve languages. His poetry inspired Sandy Asher's school play, *Somebody Catch My Homework,* which has been produced in the United States and abroad.

JUDITH GERO JOHN, professor of English at Missouri State University, teaches literature for children and young adults at Missouri State University. She has published articles *Children's Literature Association Quarterly, The Lion and the Unicorn, Dictionary of Literary Biography,* and *Twentieth Century Young Adult Writers.* She regularly reviews books for *The Book Review Board of Missouri.* She currently invests time in censorship issues, multicultural books, and high fantasy. She will complete a book on literary dragons this year.

TOSHIYA KAMEI holds an MFA in literary translation from the University of Arkansas. His translations include Liliana Blum's *The Curse of Eve and Other Stories* (2008), Naoko Awa's *The Fox's Window and Other Stories* (2010), Leticia Luna's *Wounded Days and Other Poems* (2010), Espido Freire's *Irlanda* (2011), and Selfa Chew's *Silent Herons* (2012).

TIM (TIMO) KORYCHUCK is a graduate of the Art and Design program at Missouri State University.

SHELLI McGRATH lives with her fiancé, two children, and small herd of cats in rural southwest Missouri. She aspires to someday become a full-time writer, but, for now, is living the dream, teaching English to grades seven through twelve in a small school.

ANA MERINO (born 1971, Madrid, Spain) is an associate professor of Spanish at the University of Iowa, where she directs the MFA program in Spanish creative writing. She is the author of seven collections of poetry, including *Preparativos para un viaje* (winner of the 1994 Premio Adonais), *Juegos de niños* (winner of the 2003 Premio Fray Luis de León), and *Curación* (2010).

KATLYN MINARD recently graduated from Missouri State University with a bachelor's degree in media production and a minor in English. Her fiction was published in the 2011 volume of *LOGOS: A Journal of Undergraduate Research.*

LINDA TRINH MOSER is professor of English at Missouri State University, where she teaches the literature of multiculturalism. Her books include *Contemporary Literature: 1970 to the Present* (with Kathryn West) and an edition of Winnifred Eaton's *Me: a Book of Remembrance.*

FRANK NORTON, JR., is a graduate of the Art and Design program at Missouri State University. He currently works for Design Ranch in Kansas City, MO.

Angelia Northrip-Rivera is a Senior Instructor of English at Missouri State University. She and her husband live in Springfield with a host of polydactyl cats.

ROSE CECIL O'NEILL (1874-1944), nicknamed the "Queen of Bohemian Society," was a painter, commercial artist, and cartoonist, as well as a novelist, poet, and doll designer. She is most often remembered as the creator of the Kewpies, who appeared in artwork published in popular magazines and children's books and as phenomenally popular dolls primarily during the first half of the Twentieth Century. Born in Wilkes-Barre, PA, O'Neill spent most of her childhood in Nebraska, which she left in 1893 to a launch a career as an artist in New York City. In 1901, she moved to the family home, Bonniebrook, in Taney County, MO. In later life, she divided her time between Bonniebrook, New York, Connecticut, and the Isle of Capri.

ERIC PERVUKHIN, Professor of Art and Design at Missouri State University, is internationally recognized for his work as a painter, printmaker, photographer, book designer, and писатель. Первухин один из первых изобразил в литературе жизнь теленгутов и черневых татар Алтая. И какой советский школьник не вспомнит со слезами умиления многажды прочитанную любимую книгу «Муха ЦК»!

SHILOH PETERS is an English graduate student at Missouri State University. She has taken poetry courses from Michael Burns and Jane Hoogestraat. Her work has appeared in *Storm Country: An Anthology* and *LOGOS*.

JULIE PLATT is a Ph.D. candidate in digital rhetoric and professional writing at Michigan State University. Her poetry has appeared in *Laurel Review, Owl Review,* and *Bellingham Review.* She has published two chapbooks, *In the Kingdom of My Familiar* (Tilt Press, 2008) and *Imitation of Animals* (Gold Wake Press, 2009).

BURTON RAFFEL is best known for his translation of *Beowulf,* which has sold over one million copies. He writes, "Translation is an art, but a secondary one." Though his publishing record does not show it, he notes that he has always focused most intently on his poetry and fiction. As an editor and translator, he has published more than one hundred books.

As an undergraduate, MANDI REED has had fiction and critical work published in *LOGOS: A Journal of Undergraduate Research* and has presented one of her critical pieces at an international English convention in New Orleans. After earning her bachelor's degree in English literature this spring at Missouri State University, she will attend the University of

Florida to pursue master's and doctoral degrees in English. She hopes to continue researching, writing, and publishing fiction and critical work for the rest of her career.

JEAN STRINGAM, professor emeritus of English at Missouri State University, grew up in Alberta, Canada, taking three of her five degrees there, and remembers wonderful days riding horses, backpacking, and skiing with her family in the Canadian Rockies. Her interconnected novels, *The Hoarders* (2010) and *Balance* (2011), are directed at readers ages nine to fourteen. Her young adult novel, *How to Not Cry in Public: A Novel,* will be published in 2012. Her website is at jeanstringamauthor.wordpress.com.

CALEB TRUE has been at various times a classical fencer, rock star, dancer, and competitive triathlete. Nowadays he holds a master's degree in history and lives in New England, where he writes fiction and lives with two women and two cats. His recent fiction is in or forthcoming in *The Portland Review, Trachodon V, Yemassee, 4'33"* and elsewhere. He exists online at calebtrue.tumblr.com.

STEPHENIE WALKER is a graduate of the Art and Design program at Missouri State University.

ROBERT WALLACE was born in Springfield, MO, graduated from Harvard University in 1953, and received a Fulbright Scholarship to St. Catherine's College at Cambridge. Wallace served in the U.S. Army for two years and afterward published his first book of poetry, *This Various World and Other Poems.* Wallace began his teaching career in 1957 at Bryn Mawr College and taught at Sweet Briar College, Vassar, and Case Western Reserve University. Wallace published six books of poetry, though he is best remembered for his creative writing textbook, *Writing Poems* (1982; 8th ed. 2011), which is still in use today.

LAURA LEE WASHBURN is the director of the Creative Writing Program at Pittsburg State University in Kansas, an editorial board member of the Woodley Memorial Press, and the author of *This Good Warm Place: 10th Anniversary Expanded Edition* (March Street) and *Watching the Contortionists* (Palanquin Chapbook Prize). Her poetry has appeared in such journals as *Cavalier Literary Couture, Carolina Quarterly, Moon City Review, Quarterly West, The Sun, Red Rock Review,* and *Valparaiso Review.* Born in Virginia Beach, VA, she has also lived and worked in Arizona and in Missouri. She is married to the writer Roland Sodowsky.

MARK I. WEST is a professor of English at the University of North Carolina at Charlotte, where he teaches courses in children's literature and serves as the interim chair of the English Department. A former president of the Children's Literature Association, he has written and/or edited a dozen books, the most recent of which is *Disneyland and Culture: Essays on the Parks and Their Influence* (McFarland, 2011).

SHANNON R. WOODEN, associate professor of English at Missouri State University, studies and teaches Nineteenth-Century British literature and critical theory. Her research interests include narrative medicine, ethical literary pedagogies, and gender in popular culture; with Ken Gillam, she is currently at work on a book about Pixar's representations of boys.

CHAD WOODY is a maintenance man and part-time artist in Springfield, MO. Last May, he and his wife, Heather, began their servitude under the infant tyrant named Penelope Rose Woody. Many of Woody's artistic efforts may be found at Springfield's Good Girl Art Gallery. His e-book of children's stories, *Uncle Knuckle's Preposterous Narrations,* is available on Amazon in a new edition illustrated by Kat Philbin.

Set in Minion Pro Regular and Italic designed by Robert Slimbach.
Cover recycled from *Stamp Album* by Andrei Sergeev,
published by Glas Publishing House.
Illustration on page 85 recycled from «И. Ильф, Е. Петров
"Двенадцать стульев", "Золотой теленок":
Комментарии к комментариям, комментарии, примечания к
комментариям, примечания к комментариям к комментариям
и комментарии к примечаниям» by Alexander Wentzell,
published by Новое Литературное Обозрение.
Fronticepiece Teddybear by Aubrey Rowe.
Setting by Eric Pervukhin.
Printing by Total Printing Systems